The Flower Game

FLEUR COWLES

in which nearly two hundred friends of the author
replied from many corners of the world
to her invitation to name the ten flowers they would
want to take with them if banished to a desert island
—but one where any and every flower would grow,
regardless of season or soil

William Morrow and Company, Inc.
New York   1983

By the same author

Tiger Flower
Lion and Blue
Romany Blue
Love of Tiger Flower
The Case of Salvador Dali
Bloody Precedent
Friends and Memories
All Too True

Library of Congress Catalog Card Number: 82–62541
ISBN: 0–688–02055–0

Printed in the United States of America

First U.S. Edition
1 2 3 4 5 6 7 8 9 10

CONTENTS

PAINTINGS
BY FLEUR COWLES

To Tom

INTRODUCTION

Loving and needing flowers as much as I do, how could my mind and heart survive without them if I were banished to a hypothetical 'desert' island? What flowers would make life bearable? And what would other people choose if they were in the same predicament? To find out, I invented the Flower Game. I asked nearly two hundred friends around the world to play it with me – to visualize an island which, in an unlikely event, could become their home . . . an island so enchanted that no ordinary condition of growth would exist: any and all flowers would live together, regardless of season or soil. A utopia of beautiful co-existence away from a world often ugly and divided.

The answers came from Japan, South Africa, Europe, Australia, the United States and all the other Americas. Many varities of flowers, it turned out, would have to make the trip to the idyllic island. Each reply revealed something about the person, a hint of character and of taste and, occasionally, a glimpse into childhood. Some responses were right to the point: I had asked for a list and a list was sent. Others wrote about their choices, some chattily, some poetically, as if talking the idea over with me face-to-face. The Earl of Dudley responded in the elegant verse with which this book is opened, exactly as he wrote it. The opera singer Beverly Sills sent me another sort of rhyme: her answer is in amusing and highly personal doggerel. A few, like Bernard Levin, Zubin Mehta, Victor Borge, Dorothy Stickney, Viscount Eccles, Clare Booth Luce, Stanley Marcus and the late Graham Sutherland had a love affair with one or two flowers – no more: they neither wanted nor needed others.

The *rose* flashed into prominence, eventually becoming the most wanted and thus the most beloved of all flowers *anywhere*, with good reason: the rose grows in any soil, recognizes no boundaries and is apparently impervious to all geography except the Arctic zones. I once went to pick a rose in a lush tropical garden in Cuernavaca, Mexico. It was a remarkable rose, so full-blown, so fragrant, so pink – I'd never seen one more beautiful. After many, many years I am still haunted by its memory because a huge black tarantula spider sat, immovable, on its beautiful petals. I couldn't pick it and it was hard not to faint.

In degrees of popularity, that other ubiquitous English symbol, the modest geranium, didn't fare as well as I had expected.*

* See p. 121 for a list of the top flowers chosen, in order of their popularity.

Despite its ever-present residency in window boxes and the fact that it is the uncontested pride of royal and public gardens as well as the tiniest of suburban plots, it was low on the list. Which recalls an unforgettable comment made to me years ago by the English chauffeur of a friend with whom I was riding. We were going by the then not-yet-finished concrete and glass monument to America's strength and power designed by Edward Durrell Stone, the American Embassy in London's Grosvenor Square (where there is not a flower in sight). The chauffeur, wishing to pay a compliment to me, his American passenger, turned around with a wide beam and asked: 'Won't that be a beautiful place when it's finished – when hundreds of window boxes will be added, filled with geraniums?'

Honour-bound to make my own 'desert' island list, like so many of the others, I discovered how hurtful it was to choose only ten flowers and to neglect the numberless others which, in ordinary circumstances, I'd be sad to leave out of my own Sussex or Spanish gardens.

My island, though lonely (I detest being alone) would at least be lovely if I could bring my favourite 'cottage-type' flowers to mass in a warming display around my hut/tent/shelter (whichever of these structures I could manage to build in my normal state of technical helplessness). A theme helped me narrow the choice: 'Remembrance of things past', a rallying point to evoke tangible images of my other life. What anecdotes, conversations and experiences would come to mind, what mental pictures would accompany each flower? Such an *etagère* of chosen memories might temper my loneliness.

Rebecca West once told me that Conrad had written: 'It is the mark of an inexperienced man not to believe in luck' and, wise as he was, he never wrote wiser words. Because I want luck to follow me wherever I go, I'd have to start with a fortunate little field flower, the pink *clover*. The greatest luck would be to produce a four-leafed one, and I could spend time in this happy search.

Though the rest of the list is at random, the *snowdrop* had to come next because of its frankly sentimental connection. Every year of my marriage (there are twenty-seven), the very first snowdrop which pushes through the ground in our garden (and, often, through the snow) is immediately found by my husband, who puts this tiny, touching offering in my hand. I once discovered to my delight that a similar tiny white flower meant the same to the late King Paul of Greece. I was sitting in the chintze-filled drawing-room of their private royal residence, Tatoi, outside Athens, having been invited to dinner. I came early and was quite alone when the tall, wonderfully genial king strode in from a walk in the woods. Not seeing me buried in the low sofa before the fireplace, he made straight for the chimney piece where he placed a very tiny object,

FLEUR '82

FLEUR·82

FLEUR 82

safely out of sight. Spotting me, he smiled broadly and rushed off to change from khaki shorts to suitable dress for dinner. By the time he returned, Queen Frederika and I were already absorbed in talk but I saw him reach for the mysterious object on the chimney piece to place it on the end table by her side. Only when she had turned and held it up (and flashed her famous, affectionate smile at him) did I realize that the tiny thing which had come indoors inside that large hand was a white wild flower. A single snowdrop? A violet? A Star of Jerusalem? It didn't matter. What did matter was that he, too, had the habit of picking the first one for the same tender ceremony.

I'd have to have *tulips* on my island to remind me of entrenched visual images from my life. I'd remember the famous public Gardens of Keukenhof in Holland which I first saw on an unusual trip.* Four of us, guests of Felix Guepin, were flown from London to Holland in a private plane – low, low, low over vast parkland of acres and acres of tulips of every imaginable size, colour and variety – a dazzling carpet. Later we landed and walked through the gardens and then went on to visit tulip growers. There and then I learned to understand the drama of profusion of a single flower. Tulips would conjure up a London sight I love: driving down the Mall which leads to Buckingham Palace – thousands of tulips, all brilliant red and equal in size, very tall, very neat, very dramatic, were always planted in spring in the gardens just before the palace, preceding red summer geraniums. The weeping crabapple tree between our house and barn in Sussex always had the companionship of the tiny red species Kaufmanniana tulips planted under its blossom-laden limbs: I'd like to recall that delicious sight. Below our windows, other multi-coloured, many-petalled cottage tulips brought a slash of colour to the pinkish-red tiles of our sixteenth-century house.

The *pansy*, tiny, vulnerable, lovable, would recall the pansy-people who populate one of our most admired paintings by the French primitive painter, André Beauchant. A dozen or more beguiling pansy faces are collected in a group which looks intently from the canvas. The palest of blue pansies edge both sides of long rows of Elizabeth of Glamis roses leading to our Sussex door. Because the pansy is one of Queen Elizabeth the Queen Mother's favourites, they would remind me of someone very dear to me.

The *tuberose* would bring my home in Spain into focus. An ancient Moorish cistern, which was unexpectedly discovered under the Roman castle I restored in the centre of Spain, has given us plenty of water for a garden – despite the harshness elsewhere in

---

* The rest of the trip would come to mind too: that journey from England to Holland ended days later in an evening at the Rijksmuseum in Amsterdam. The museum had been re-opened (after-hours) to give us a private, leisurely stroll through a magical place.

the dry Extremadura Province. Water brought 'instant' growth to the flowers and trees I planted in the Moorish garden (after I dynamited away the huge boulders which were there). I grew tuberoses discreetly but plentifully at the far end of the garden, for their fragrance. I used to place one (and only one) to welcome guests just inside the entrance and a few stems always came back to England with me to use in the same way, to let their heady fragrance drift gently through our house. Yes, a tuberose would always say 'Spain' to me.

I would have to have the humble field *daisy*, that everyday flowering wonder which obviously finds the fields more attractive than cultivated gardens. I'd choose the daisy because of its unaffected simplicity and because it would bring back instant-childhood. I still remember the joy of walking knee-deep in the fields near our home in the United States, arms full of daisies. I also appreciate the way that the daisy accommodates one by growing into huge clumps after but a few have been planted. Also, for my unmechanized mind, the daisy remains my sort of computer: I still count petal by petal to get the answers to searing (if hypothetical) questions.

White *jasmine* climbs up the pinky-beige stone walls of our Spanish home; there I planted it in profusion so it could find its way to the bedroom windows in both towers. And, often, I'd pick a small handful of short-stemmed ones from the vines to float in a low bowl so that the fragrance permeated the room. On my island, I could do the same (even popping in a pink rose). The question of flower containers would, of course, arise but it wouldn't trouble me. I'm totally capable with my fingers and could make something from whatever was available – starting with the largest shells from the seaside and the coconuts from the palm trees I'd expect to find on my island. I could weave basket containers (and put them to use after working out a way to *line* them).

Of course I'd need the *rose* – because every rose that grows is a rose I love. Because, looking into one, I'd instantly recall the literature I've enjoyed . . . Shakespeare, who wrote more constantly of the rose than of any other flower in all his plays . . . I'd recall Katherine Mansfield, one of my favourite authors, with *In the Garden* . . . Katherine Anne Porter's literary essay on the rose written for *Flair* magazine which I created and edited in the United States . . . André Maurois' *Climat* . . . and others, others . . . But even before my mind became involved with memories of things *written* about the rose, two other senses, *sight* and *smell*, would have to be engaged. Every painter I love, if worth his salt, has painted the rose, from a tiny one in a Madonna's hand, to a Fantin-Latour portrait of many roses. Brueghel and all the Dutch and French and Roman and Spanish painters always included the rose in their flower masterpieces. Redouté paintings without a rose? Impossible.

The rose sadly lost its fragrance in recent years when horticulturists tended not to worry about scent when they were developing new strains. Or couldn't they do both? Luckily, scented roses are once again being created and the old fashioned ones which never lost their smell are not only back in fashion but firmly entrenched as favourites in catalogues. I'd only have such roses on my island. The Fleur Cowles rose, which is fragrant, would remind me that Gregory & Son, rose growers of Nottingham, named an extraordinarily beautiful new florabunda rose for me (what a lovely form of immortality), a rose which I would swear I'd seen all my life in Fantin-Latour's paintings: plump, pale (off-white with a blush of pink), romantic. If I could have two roses and count them as one, I'd also choose the deep, deep, dark velvety-red, nearly black rose called Etoile de Hollande, whose fragrance is haunting and whose colour would inject a brooding beauty in my otherwise bright garden.

Of course, I'd have to bring another *wild flower* besides the clover – and it could be any one in nature's magical world: a tiny wild orchid or, more touchingly, the cowslip, that disappearing friend of the field. Or the buttercup, which would spread out and produce a bright yellow carpet. Or the primula, to remind me of the hedgerows at home. Or the dandelion, that much maligned flower which no one has yet succeeded in eradicating, though millions have tried. Or cow parsley which, once planted, grows so furiously that it needs no help in spreading its lace quite wildly. I agree with Sylvia Earle, who played this Flower Game with me,* that 'If human beings were characteristically three inches high, they would find that even field grasses have an awesome beauty.'

The *lily-of-the-valley* has a special place in my heartbank, for it is the flower my husband always sends me when they are available. Their whiteness, fragrance and tiny size have always moved me.

Like so many of my players, I'm going to cheat just a little and name the flowers I would mourn. First of all, the *nasturtium*, to remind me of a visit when I was a little girl and was taken to dine in Long Island, where I saw this simple flower used with such panache. The house was a converted barn one entered on a level above the rest of the vast room stretched out below. There was a fireplace ablaze with logs so large they seemed like tree trunks; directly in front of it was a five-foot square coffee table and, placed on it, a copper bowl at least thirty inches across. It was tightly packed with hundreds of yellow, red and orange nasturtiums, with a ring of their leaves curling round the bowl. Not even the roaring fire could compete with this dancing blaze of colour. Yes, I would want nasturtiums to grow (and glow) beneath the foot of every tree

* See page 47.

I'd find there, to climb as high as possible – and to pick for tight, merry little bouquets.

Then the *anemone*, for its intensity; the *Iceland poppy*, whose large crinkly-crêpe petals I have always enjoyed painting (as well as the wild variety which would give me a bright red backdrop); the luscious fat pink *peony*, because of a yearning to pack some tightly into any sort of container. In another corner of my mind there would always be a *phalenopsis orchid*, pure, innocent, not at all like its relatives (just one thin bending stem with a shock of white flowers at its end, which I recently introduced into my greenhouse); the *violet*, which I learned after years of frustration to keep alive (and I could even do so on my island) by turning them face down in water overnight to let them drink through the flowers. I'd like big, fat, white, fragrant *stock*, which goes on blooming for ever. The *sunflower*, chosen symbol of Louis XIV's reign, could also be the garden's bold sentinel. The *protea*, enormous and unreal, which normally lives in South Africa, especially those with white chalk-dusted pink petals which I find the most beautiful. Instead of dying, proteas turn into fascinating dry flowers and stay on for months and months. I often paint them and have used the single white one as a motif in design (one is a tall pink *papier-maché* lamp). The *frangipani* would remind me of a brief but priceless stop on the island of Bali many, many years ago. Last but not least, I'm upset by having left out the white *lilac*, friend of all romantics. If on my island, they'd help me dream.

One sober thought is inescapable: I'd like to find on the island, to cherish and care for, one of the world's fast-disappearing wild flowers, perhaps the wild orchid which, like thousands of others, is in such danger today.

Fleur Cowles

DILMUN

(Dilmun was the Garden of Eden of the Sumerian creation myth. Some archaeologists ascribe a prehistorical background to the myth, and locate Dilmun on the island of Bahrein.)

I will have *daffodil* to smile
And congregate my lonely isle.
Hydrangea bursting with delight
Will range with pink and blue and white
Against the breeze; behind their screen
The island will be decked in green
As *clover* flowers everywhere.
Lilac's scent will fill the air.
The fair *camellia* will dream
Of love. And blush. Flames gleam
Where the *azaleas* blaze. A glow
Of fiercer fire where *paeonies* will grow.
Then, to refresh, a glimpse of white and gold
Where the sweet perfumed *lily* will unfold.
I must have *clematis*. And so will make
A shelter on whose sides the flower may break.
And yet my heart's not beating till it knows
That it shall fill my senses with the *rose*.

Dudley

The Flower Game

Rupert Allen

LOS ANGELES

Publicist, once an editor of *Look* and *Flair* magazines

My most favourite is the *paeony* – for its heady fragrance, its lushness and its beautiful colouring, whether it be snow white with flecks of bold red, deep red or pale pink. Chinese artists over the centuries have been in love with it, and quite rightly so!

My second choice is the *lilac*, whether purple or white. Its fragrance again makes it a favourite with me, plus its delicacy. Moreover, I am sentimentally attached to it because of the huge and very old lilac stand we had at my father's place, Wind Haven, Missouri; one stand of white and another of purple, and they were big enough for us, as children, to romp under the blossoms with our dogs.

Third, the *rose*. Again, for a variety of delicious and heady scents and magnificent colours. Of course, it has a special significance for me, since it was a symbol of *Flair* magazine.

Fourth, *lily-of-the-valley*. Again, the scent and the delicacy of the blossoms. Quite rightly, the French say it brings good luck if you give or receive *muguets* on May Day. Moreover, lily-of-the-valley is really the *fleur-de-lis* on coats-of-arms – my grandmother had the right to use it on hers through her French antecedents, including the family of Henry IV.

Agapanthus, the flower of the Nile, is my fifth choice, whether rich blue or snow white. The flowers are graceful and yet regal with beautifully tapering leaves.

Then the *iris*, for its glorious shape and delicate colourings – from the Siberian and Japanese varieties to the back garden purple, yellow and white ones. It, too, has a delightful scent.

The next one – speaking of scent – is the velvety white *tuberose*, with a heavy fragrance that can be overpowering if you are caught in a small room with a number of them.

I would then choose the *nasturtium*, partly because its name in French is so beautiful – *capucine*. Also, its leaves are so good in salad; its blossoms always have bright and invigorating colours, beautiful in form and delicate in scent.

Then *geraniums*, because they are heartening with their bright and wild colours, because they will grow anywhere as long as they have sun and because they can cheer up the gloomiest of neighbourhoods and alleyways.

Wisteria – I don't think anybody could ever know how truly beautiful wisteria can be until they've seen it tumbling over old Tuscan villas and walls on the way from Fiesole. Whether white or purple, it is a true reward of spring. It is interesting to me that wisteria, like lilac and agapanthus, come in only two colours: white and a deep bluish purple.

My last (even if it is the eleventh) is the *bluebell*. A mass of bluebells spilling across the ground in the woods on an English spring day is a sight hard to believe. They truly are the bridge between the earth and sky.

Jorge Amado

BAHIA, SALVADOR
Brazilian author

It happens that we (Zelia and I) have run away from the city and have isolated ourselves from everything and everyone, in our beach house twenty minutes away from town. This is a very beautiful place where we have hidden ourselves so that I can write my books in peace; we have no telephone here and no one dares show up without an invitation!

I am giving you below the names of the flowers I like best: *roses*; *violets*; *lilies*; *caryofiláceas* (Dianthus plumarius); *bougainvilleas*; *forget-me-nots*; *daisies*; *carnations*; *gardenias*; *orchids*.

Unfortunately, I cannot have these flowers which I care for so much in my garden at the beach for, due to this particular climate, only coconuts and cactus grow well here.

Mrs Walter Annenberg

WASHINGTON, DC
Wife of US Ambassador to the
Court of St James, 1969–75

What ten flowers I'd choose from the vast varieties I love? It wasn't easy. After some thought I propose the following:

Orchids (phalconopies, vandas, cymbidiums, cattlyeas); *paeonies*; *chrysanthemums*; *rubrum lilies*; *carnations*; *hydrangeas*; *roses*; *anthericum*; *lily-of-the-valley*; *begonias*.

Mme Kazu Aso

TOKYO
Lady-in-waiting to the Empress of Japan

Roses; *daffodils*; *iris*; *sweet peas*; *marguerites*; and, if flowering trees and shrubs are permitted: *cherries*; *camellias*; *rhododendrons*; *forsythia*; *spiraea*.

Carole Austen

LONDON
French couturier

Lys – France; *coquelicot* – the country in France; *muguet* – the house of Dior; *tulipe* – forms and colours; *marguerite* – simple, decorative; *azalée* – pure white; *zinnia* – colours, exotisme; *chrysanthème* – charme; *jasmin* – parfum; *camellia* – royal England.

Lauren Bacall

NEW YORK CITY
Stage and screen actress

Before I had a country house my favourite flowers were *anemones*, *freesias*, *gardenias* and *orchids*. These are all still among my favourites and I'd want to have them on my 'desert' island; but I'd also have to have my homegrown *roses* with their natural scent, as well as *lilacs* and *forget-me-nots*.

I now have a very English garden – one or more of everything I like – and it runs mostly to pinks, mauves and whites. I'd want to make my 'desert' garden as much like this as possible, and I'd plant *butterfly bushes* to attract butterflies and hummingbirds and *bee balm* for the bees. Even if I hadn't planted them myself, I'd have chosen every one and so I'd feel as though I had.

I've become a bird freak in addition to all else, and find watching plants grow and flowers bloom is glorious!

Jack Baker

CARPINTERIA, CALIFORNIA
Gardener and floral painter

The brave and beautiful *daffodil* – the epitome of the renaissance of spring; the *nasturtium* – the fantasy flower of our childhood, lily-pad leaves which hold jewel-like drops of water, painted clown faces and tails filled with honey make it a delight to all the senses; the tiny *hibiscus* species found in the Alakai Swamp on the island of Kaiwai, shaped and marked like exquisite jungle insects; *pansies* are people; an old tea *rose* of pale pink – simple in form, exquisite in texture, haunting in fragrance; *matilija poppy* – the astonishing tree poppies native to the California foothills, the purity of their crêpe crinkled white petals, golden stamens and intoxicating fragrance make them magic; *delphiniums* – I like blue!; simple country *pinks* blooming in a Sicilian rock wall; Louis XIV, the Sun King's choice of the *sunflower* for the floral symbol of his reign was brilliant – was there ever a flower more of an absolute monarch? The blossom of the *plumeria*, a reflection of the splendour of the tropics.

Betty Beale

WASHINGTON, DC
Columnist

My favourite ten: *roses* – especially coral pink ones; *paeonies* – for full-bodied beauty; *anemones* – for sheer splashes of colour; *tuberoses* – for rich fragrance; *freesias* – delicate petals, colour and fragrance; *bougainvillea* – for spilling its redness over a wall; *camellias* – pink ones for porcelain-like perfection; *lily-of-the-valley* – for their joyous little bells and fragrance; *impatiens* – coral pink, because they get more and more abundant and never stop blooming; *tulips* – the big double ones in a variety of colours.

Sir Cecil Beaton

SALISBURY, WILTSHIRE
The late artist, writer and photographer

Any large white *orchid* of any variety, so long as it is white. (I have grown some and they are a great delight!); white *paeony*; dark red *rose*; white *rose*; pink *rose*; *lily-of-the-valley*; *auratum lily*; white *marguerites*; white *geraniums*; *clematis*.

The Duchess of Bedford

PARIS
Socialite

Lilium speciosum rubrum; *tuberose*; *stephanotis*; *magnolia* and *magnolia stellata*; *gardenia*; *jasmine*; *delphinium*; yellow *tulips* or pink and green parrot *tulips*; Peace *rose* or Prima Ballerina or Iceberg; *laburnum*; pink *hyacinth*.

Baroness G Bentinck

PARIS
Widow of Dutch Ambassador
to the Court of St James, 1958–63

Poppies; *cornflowers*; *orchids*; *violets*; white *roses*; *tulips*; *daisies*; *cherry blossoms*; *forget-me-nots*; black *Turkish tulips*; *lily-of-the-valley*.

Roloff Beny

ROME
Photographer and author

On my 'desert' island perhaps I could settle for only *ferns*, slender *bulrushes*, *papyrus* and *wild crocus* to herald the spring! However, given a more sybaritic range, I would joyfully include *tulips*, wild and frivolous as they come – because, as they mature, their serpentine stems weave baroque patterns, unlike the most hated, aggressive gladioli which (along with florists' rigid and forced carnations) are highest on my hate list.

Yes, give me the great *geranium tree bushes* which flourish on the island of Crete; all *poppies*, which surge indestructibly from the classical ruined amphitheatres of the Mediterranean and are equally happy growing waist-high in the wheat fields of Lombardy.

In the forest on my island, should I be so fortunate, I ask for the *dogwood* and the *maple* which chromatically herald the seasons in my native Canada. On my one little lake, the long-stemmed *Persian lotus* which I love on the Mordab would be ideal with my papyrus grove.

I'm over-running but in the garden of my rush hut, *paeonies* and single mauve *lilac* must be planted, blooming together to be joined in terracotta jars which will grace my long wooden trattoria table, performing as the drafting board of my dreams – of course, many of them dreams of my friends.

Candice Bergen

NEW YORK CITY
Actress, writer and photographer

Here is my list of ten flowers: *paeonies, rubrum lilies, any* kind of *orchid, violets, lily-of-the-valley, gardenias, jasmine* (night-blooming), *wisteria, lilacs, field daisies.*

Flowers to see *and* smell – by day and night – that bloom underfoot and hang overhead, plus a few insect escorts – butterflies and caterpillars, the odd ladybug – for company. But, basically, I would be thrilled with flowers and birds of every kind and colour . . . except gladioli and birds of paradise. Sometimes you have to put your foot down.

Victor J Bergeron

SAN FRANCISCO
Restaurateur

My favourite flowers, which I used to grow, are: great big *pansies*; wild *primroses* (or were they wild *violets*?) *Californian poppies*; Bewitched *roses*; *cymbidium orchids*; *primulas*; lily-of-the-valley; double *marguerites*; *adelphiums*; *tiger lilies*.

Mrs Barry Bingham

GLENVIEW, KENTUCKY
Wife of proprietor of the *Louisville Courier*

My selection of ten favourites is a difficult one. One would like to include foxgloves and pinks, so beloved by Beatrix Potter; Parma violets one remembers pinned in one's mother's furs (the smell!); savage nasturtiums and zinnias; and bluettes or Quaker Ladies, which carpeted the Virginia pine woods of one's childhood. But for flowers, and the *only* ones, to live with I feel the list must be less idiosyncratic and more useful for enlivening the interior of the shack on the island. So . . . I attach my considered list: white *hyacinths*; *syringa* (French hybrid lilacs, white; *lily-of-the-valley*; *aquilegia*; (double long-spurred hybrid columbines); *paeonies*; *anemone*; *japonica* (windflowers, pink and white); *sweet peas*; *delphiniums* (Pacific hybrids); *phlox*; *roses* (Garden Party).

Molly Bishop (Lady George Scott)

LONDON
Portrait painter

'On an imaginary "desert" island, with ten of my favourite flowers!'
Far too few, of course, but what fantasies proliferate – and questions.

For instance: would one have to be alone? (I hope not) And would one have to stay there indefinitely? (Oh, I *do* hope not!) But, in either case, I'd have to be reminded of my English garden or go mad like Ben Gunn on Treasure Island. Even if I could escape this fate or, better still, just be a visitor, I think I'd still prefer to have my long-beloved faithful blooms (so eagerly awaited each year) around me.

Perhaps that sounds insular and unimaginative (by the way, we are told that any and all flowers will bloom there so it won't really be 'desert', thank goodness) – but wait! Starting with spring, have you never experienced the joy of discovering the first *pheasant's eye narcissus* growing in long orchard grass? Not the large cultivated kind with 'eyes' of orange tissue paper but the true old-fashioned ones with their intoxicating scent.

Scent plays an all-important part in my choice of favourites. All must breathe fragrance.

Some are wild; I feel so honoured when they appear in my garden of their own accord and bloom in such casual abundance – like for instance sweet rocket and foxgloves. My next choice would be *lily-of-the-valley*, shyly peeping from their thickly crowding twin leaves with their unique fragrance delighting my springtime nose, hungry for summer scents.

Soon the *philadelphus'* fresh, orangey perfume would waft from starry white blossoms in dark green foliage and perhaps, as this is a fantasy garden, I might be spared the annual scourge of the hay-fever contained in its pollen.

And could I be granted a bonus in the form of an April blackbird crooning from its depths his creamy, leisured phrases of bird-jazz blues? My own garden is almost a bird sanctuary and I'd miss the songs of my linnets, finches and warblers as well as our faithful thrushes, blackbirds and robins, and the swoop and twitter of summer swallows.

I'd like to gather the *cowslip*'s sweet-smelling cap-and-bells, now so rare on the downs, and have a bower of white scented *jasmine* and climbing *roses*, Albertine perhaps – smelling of sweet apples – to sit under. Nearby I might have a hedge of musk rose penelope, her scent exactly like my mother's best cold cream (attar of roses, I suppose) when I was a child; is it cheating to assume that all roses count as one species?

I would need Keats' wealth of globèd *paeonies'* to luxuriate among – the palest pink stripey ones tumbling in scented profusion over daisy-starred grass (those *daisies* whose innocent heads are so ruthlessly mown off by British gardeners!). And could I have a mass of grey-foliaged laced *pinks* to cushion my feet, with their delicious smell of clover and spices, looking like neat little girls in clean print dresses?

And then a riot of *phloxes* to intoxicate me with the brilliant coral, crimson, white and purple and their slightly tobacco-y perfume, evocative of late summer when foliage is mellowing and harvest is just around the corner.

An added luxury would be a *buddleia* with its velvety spires of purple florets breathing honey for every kind of butterfly.

I do hope trees don't count in the ten, because I'd hope to find an apple tree to 'lean down low' as in Linden Lea, and lime trees full of bloom to be another 'haunt of bees' (like Keats' musk rose). I couldn't do without the bees and their comforting sound.

And that must be ten or more, without mentioning lilies or nicotiana or lilac, all of which I'd miss dreadfully.

One final boon I would ask: that all flowers might be pest and disease-free! If I could be spared the endless mixing, spraying and squirting that beshrew the gardener's life, 'then wilderness were Paradise enow'.

Earl Blackwell

NEW YORK CITY
Social chronicler

Jasmine; *bougainvillea*; *hyacinth*; *lily-of-the-valley*; *paeony*; pink *carnation*; pink *rose*; *dogwood*; *cherry blossom*; *daisy* and *nasturtium*.

Baron Böel

BRUSSELS
Belgian socialite
famed for his garden

Odoroglossum orchid; *arum lily*; *azalée*; *cyclamen*; *iris*; *mimosa*; *lilas*; *cythise* (laburnum); *freesia*; *camellia*.

Victor Borge

CONNECTICUT
Musical satirist

Which ten flowers would I choose to take to a lonely island? My answer: ten *tulips*.

Juan Bourguignon

MADRID
Horticulturist and florist

Every flower, just opening and giving a lovely perfume at midday, to me is beautiful. My ten whispering, perfumed flowers to put on this beautiful island: *violets*; *lily-of-the-valley*; *daffodils* and *tulips*; *lilacs*; red *roses* (floribundas); *viburnum* (snowballs); *vallotas* (like nerines); *nasturtiums*; *thalictrum*; *alpine carnations* (mignardise).

Mrs Kingman Brewster

NEWHAVEN, CONNECTICUT
Wife of US Ambassador
to the Court of St James, 1977–81

The total lack of botanical names will, I fear, tell you nearly all about my taste in flowers! Is it a cheat to add lilac and beach palm to the list? They do blossom gloriously and one might need shade. So . . . for what it is worth, the list: *paeonies*; *narcissi*; *lily-of-the-valley*; *tulips* (especially 'striped'); *roses* (the old-fashioned, fragrant sort); *jasmine*; *anemones*; *verbena*; *lilacs*; *pinks* (again, older scented sort).

So, a shameless bouquet – making a mixture of an unsophisticated cottage-garden sort.

Mrs Evangeline Bruce

WASHINGTON, DC
Widow of US Ambassador
to the Court of St James, 1961–9

Auratum lilies; *jasmine*; Rembrandt and Viridiflora *tulips*, fringed, mottled, striped, flamed and striped; *phlox*, for the scorched smell; *hyacinths*; shrub *roses* (a lot of Variegata di Bologna and one Floribunda Evangeline Bruce); *Sweet Williams*; *tree paeonies*; *auricula*: the grey-flannel ones and the chrome-colour; the lot surrounded by a cloud of *cow parsley*.

Mrs James Callaghan

RINGMER, SUSSEX
Wife of UK Prime Minister, 1976–9

My list is simple though I didn't find it too easy to decide. However, here it is:

Primroses and wild *violets* – blue and white if that is allowed. From childhood it has always been my delight to pick them in the woods; *daffodils* – tall and tiny, pale or deep gold, in great drifts or small clumps; two more wild flowers: *bluebells* and *ragged robins* (red campions), preferably growing together; *honeysuckle*, for its scent and its beauty; I expect everyone's list will include *roses* and I must include them in mine – all kinds if allowed – but, if I must be more specific, hybrid tea bush roses; number eight, would, I think be *pansies* – they vary so and keep blooming for so long; *chrysanthemums* I love, though not their smell, again for their great variety of colour, shape and size; finally, in a hot, jungly corner, probably unsuitable for all the others, I would like to grow *orchids* – great sprays of them. P.S. Would like *sweet peas* too – so difficult.

Mme Louis Camu

AALST, BELGIUM
Owner of noted garden

Lily-of-the-valley; *sweet peas*; *paeonies*; white *Madonna lilies*; *pinks* (single dianthus); *roses*; *irises*; *ranunculus* (and other spring garden flowers but not buttercups); *nasturtiums*; *primroses*.

Elizabeth Carpenter

AUSTIN, TEXAS
Press officer to Mrs Lyndon B. Johnson
in the White House

I've just come from a lovely, heavenly spot in Mexico – San Miguel de Allende; it was certainly *not* a lonely island, but I would definitely want to take every flower I saw there if I were going to such a spot . . . I'll play your 'Flower Game', delightedly . . .

If I were selecting a floral bouquet for a lonely island, it would include the romantic flowers: *lilacs*; *anemones*; *crocuses*; yellow *roses*; *bougainvillea*; *forget-me-not*.

But my favourites, the ones I would have to have, are the lovelies – the wild flowers of Texas: *bluebonnets*; *winecups*; *Indian paintbrush*; wild *daisies*; wild *poppies* – a collage of colour and nostalgia.

Lady Carrington

AYLESBURY, BUCKINGHAMSHIRE
Wife of UK Foreign Secretary, 1979–82

I'm not likely to be happy all alone on that island but, on inadequate reflection, I think the flowers which might compensate best for the human race might be: *cyclamen* Coum; *Anemone blanda*; all sorts of *campanula*; *Narcissus triandrus* – all of which would increase and carpet the island with charming little faces and attractive leaves (the first three); *lilies*; *philadelphus* (single ones) to scent the air; water *lilies*; *paeonies*; shrub *roses*, which would remind me of England and, preferably, be scented; *camellias*.

Ernestine Carter

LONDON
Author (former women's editor
of the London *Sunday Times*)

When I started to think about that 'desert' island where everything grows, I suddenly realized that I had a longing for my garden in London. I do not exactly have agoraphobia but I do have a liking for enclosed spaces. I would therefore take with me some of the plants that I have in London with the confidence that they will grow beautifully. Especially on the 'desert' island where there will be a rampage of colour, I would keep my own garden to its usual green and white.

My garden owes its being to Lanning Roper who originally put in the screen of *hornbeam* which gives the garden its character. This grows very quickly and on the island would not need the expensive pollarding and pleaching that such screens demand in London. Mr Roper also planted the climbing *Hydrangea petiolaris* which covers one wall. This takes years to grow in London but perhaps would grow more quickly on the 'desert' island. The third wall, which I imagine will be made of a light screen of wood such as bamboo, I would plant entirely with *clematis* and I would have in the centre of the wall a semi-circle of wire to form an embrasure for eating. This too would be roofed and walled in clematis. For the clematis I would choose montana, the Duchess of Edinburgh, Marie Boisselot and amandii.

As I like plants in clumps I mass all my hydrangeas together and prefer only white lace-caps, paniculata and the paniculata praecox. These go along the wall under the climbing hydrangea. In one corner I would like a *philadelphus* bush with its charming white flowers and beautiful scent; in the other a *spiraea*, equally talented.

For white flowers, I choose *candytuft* (iberis) which, from a small beginning, seeds itself and spreads into waterfalls of chalk-white. These alternate with white *marguerites* which have the same happy facility of expanding and, of course, one must have *camellias* – two at least are splendid in white, alba and the giant. And when I was planning this tiny garden, Lanning Roper advised me to have two *box balls* which I should love to repeat; and a *hebe* sub-alpina which flowers into tiny little white blossoms and also grows into a ball. There is something very charming about these round shapes. For dramatic contrast to the smaller, sharper leaves of other plants, my favourite is *funkia* (hosta), with its sweeping foliage in an infinite variety of colour and pattern.

I have come to the end of my allocated choices and see that I have left out the scented paeonies, the white fuchsias, the choisya ternata, the hibiscus, the roses and the bulbs, anemone blanda (white splendour) and clusiana. What a small garden accommodates! I have also left out a terrace. Although in principle I could make one, in fact I know I wouldn't and I suggest marking out a rectangle along the garden wall of the hut, defined by white geraniums in pots.

This is, I know a limited garden with very little available for cutting, but I imagine that on the 'desert' island there will be a plethora of blooms so that it will be a relief to have the inside of the hut cool and bare.

MARYLAND

Botanist, past President of
American Horticulture Society

For your 'game,' the ten flowers are:

Aeschyanthus Sp: lipstick vine and relatives. The original 'I don't care plant' – absolutely hardy foliage with orange-red flowers as surprises on the branches; *Chrysanthemum morifolium*: any lace or spider type. Total action in space – on a plant with all of the control of a robot (a biological wonder and my major research plant); *Datura suaveolens*: angel's trumpet. Unique form, with flowers hanging, almost blotting the sky with the creamy texture of the trumpet; *Dicentra spectabilis*: Bleeding Heart. One of the great design forms and colours in a hardy perennial. Always delights any gardening design; *Fritillaria imperialis*: Crown Imperial. The truly one regal plant – combines history of Himalayas and Western culture – a marvel of terracotta, mauve and form; *Hibiscus schizopetalis*: species hibiscus with hanging flowers, looks just like dancers in Walt Disney's *Fantasia*: creamy-orange with magenta tipped anthers and pistils; *Osmanthus fragrans*: sweet olive. The most delightful fragrance in the world, on a coarse, deep green evergreen – flowers all winter long on my deserted isle; *paphiopedilum*: Lady Slipper. Ultimate form and colour and textures in a flower. Art shades and chaste foliage always make any setting just perfect; *Pieris japonica*: Andromeda. *Lily-of-the-valley* on evergreen shrub – great elegant beauty of ivory flowers and buds for many months of the year; *Tigridia pavonia*: shell flower. Perfect flowers for a C.B. de Mille production – colour, form and growth habit is dazzling and often neglected.

Deena Clark

WASHINGTON, DC
Columnist, *Diplomat* magazine

Shooting Star: this was my very first flower favourite. I loved it when I was a child growing up in La Jolla, swimming in the cold, clear waters of the cove and hiking on the sage-covered California hills. In those days, when I went to pick wild flowers on the slopes of Mount Soledad, I found hundreds of yellow violets with their pungent fragrance intensified by the warmth of the sun. Massive drifts of Indian paintbrush floated down canyon sides, staining the canvas of the brown slopes with their tufted crimson. But the shooting stars were my best-loved. They were so clean, so neatly designed, pointing skyward, poised like miniature rockets aimed at the cloudless blue California sky.

Shasta daisy: when I was about eight years old, I very adventurously, feeling like a pioneer, embarked on a journey. I went all alone on a street car fifteen miles due south from La Jolla to San Diego's famous Balboa Park. At the entrance to one of the stucco, bell-towered, Spanish-style buildings was a spacious square planted entirely in majestic shasta daisies. Rising from the exact centre of the field was a jet black statue of Father Junipero Serra. The impact of that black basalt sculptured figure contrasting with the blinding white and blazing yellow of the daisies has remained with me all my life.

Queen Anne's lace: Each little floweret is 'crocheted' of myriads of tiny petals to form a perfect star-like blossom. Then dozens join that original tiny nucleus to make the second perfect cluster of écru lace. Hundreds more, each in its own geometric space, come together to fashion another, larger flower. Then, suspended on its own delicate straw-like stem, each one repeats itself – like the bursts of fiery flowers that radiate from the glowing wire of a Fourth of July sparkler.

Sonia *rose*: I suppose no flower has ever surpassed the rose in popularity. It has held the heart of the world since before Homer first described 'the rosy-fingered dawn' and centuries later Redouté painted his one thousand roses for Napoleon's Josephine – the blossoms being her chief consolation in her unhappy retirement at Malmaison. My own favourite is a modern variety – the Sonia – whose blossoms glow with both orange and pink – the exact colour of a Bahamian sunset. In a bouquet a lovely surprising combination is mixing the Sonia rose with long stemmed daisies, thus uniting the symbol of love with that of innocence.

White *ginger*: I love Hawaii. I was married there in an 'arcadian' garden before a sundial and, years later, my daughter Nikia was christened at that same wedding sundial. White ginger to me is Hawaii's most heartbreakingly beautiful blossom. Its scientific name is hedychium coronarium. 'Hedychium' is from the Greek, meaning 'sweet snow'. 'Coronarium' refers to its exquisite crown of glistening white petals. A mountain dweller, it stands with regal dignity on its majestic stalk in the cool forests of Tantalus far above the city of Honolulu. The white ginger's snowy buds are gathered in the very early morning, while they are still wet with dew. When gently opened and strung into a *lei*, they form a chaste garland of unforgettable purity and perfume.

Geranium: the geranium appeals to almost all our senses. It is lovely to look at, its 'furry' leaves are pleasant to touch and it gives off a spicy fragrance. Finally, there is no sound to equal that crisp, sharp little pop when one snaps off yesterday's leaves or faded blooms. There is almost therapeutic comfort in keeping the geranium looking its tidy best. It demands no decision. The gardener cannot make a mistake – there is a built-in, natural 'snapping-off place' for separating stem and stalk.

Nasturtium: nasturtium is a graceful little trumpet, its flared 'bell' balanced unbelievably by an impossibly delicate cornucopia. As a child I discovered that a tiny bit off that slender tip would yield a drop of delicious nectar. The immaculate leaf, like a miniature lily pad, has a fascination all its own. As non-absorbent as kitchen table oilcloth, you can transform a drop of water into a glittering diamond by splashing it on that pliable circle. Several drops will combine to form quicksilver. Push a finger into that liquid nugget and it will split, then rush together again just like an alchemist's liquid mercury rolled in the palm of one's hand.

Single *paeony*: I *like* the double paeony, whose many-layered curling petals captivated Marco Polo thousands of years ago in China, but I *love* the single paeony. I think the white, with its golden yellow centre, is particularly stunning. With its single ring of only five petals which resemble crinkled chiffon, it looks like a magnificent king-sized opium poppy.

Cyclamen: cyclamen, with its heavy ruffled dark green leaves, was my mother's favourite flower. On holidays my sister and I would pool the coins we had saved to spend at the florist's shop. We raided our 'banks' (twist-top mason jars with a screwdriver-punched slot for pennies, nickels and dimes) to buy a plant whose amethyst stems seemed to support white butterflies rather than blossoms. When I was grown up I made my very first visit to Greece, where my father was born. There on the island of Corfu, in October's bright blue weather, when I climbed the heights above the curving bay of Palaeokastritsa, I came upon a mountain-top meadow completely carpeted with tiny cyclamen no more than two inches high. I never dreamed such miniatures existed! What an intense and happy surprise, while exploring the land of my own roots, to discover unexpectedly the wild ancestors of the cultivated cyclamen which gave my mother so much pleasure.

Laburnum: my final favourite, sometimes called 'golden chain', is a tree-flower resembling wisteria. Golden yellow, the laburnum blossoms hang from the branches in delicate clusters, looking like perfectly balanced natural 'mobiles'. When the breezes blow, one can almost hear the music of golden chimes.

Peter Coats

LONDON
Author, gardening authority and
Garden Editor of UK *Vogue*

My choice of flowers – on the understanding that Fleur does not count (how many people will make that sort of joke!): *rose* – because there is a greater variety and a greater mystique in roses than in any other flower; *lily* – because they are difficult to grow and make a challenge and because they are beautiful; *viola* – because they have such character and, again, are so different: some almost have human faces; *narcissus* – because there is an Oriental phrase: 'If you have two coins, spend one on bread and one on flower of Narcissus – because bread is food for the body but flower of Narcissus is food for the soul.'; *salpiglossis* – because their colour range is wider and stranger than that of any other plant; *passion flower* – for its extraordinary flower structure and for its associations; *nicotiana* – for the scent and the flowers and, if you ran out of cigarettes, you could smoke the leaves.

Only seven I fear, but there it is.

Lady Collins

LONDON
Widow of the publisher, Sir William Collins

Old fashioned *roses* – namely varieties Queen of Denmark and Chapeau de Napoléon; *sweet peas*; *Sweet Williams*; *pinks*; *auriculas*; *tulips*; autumn *crocus*; *helleborus* (Christmas roses); *delphiniums*; *paeonies*.

Sybil Connolly

DUBLIN
Couturier

Here is a list of my ten favourite flowers and the reason why: *iris reticulata*: because its construction and colouring to me are a near miracle – examining it closely would help to while away the hours on a lonely island; *Helleborus orientalis*: of all the hellebore family, this is my favourite – its colouring is so beautiful. When one lifts the slightly drooping head and sees the delicacy of pale pink and pale green smudged on to a white face, it is positively breathtaking in its gentle beauty; *Primula vulgaris*: (the ordinary common primrose one finds growing in the hedgerows of some country lanes) – such innocence as it evokes would give me hope in my loneliness, and the clear earthy smell it exudes has an unsurpassed freshness; paperwhite *narcissus*: the occupation of planting the bulbs and their slow but exciting emergence from the compost until, finally, the petals break through, is so fascinating. Then, one is almost overcome by the sweetness of their scent; *parrot tulips*: for their extravagant colours and growing habits – how could one not feel gay in the presence of such joyous abandonment? *lilac*: this tied with wisteria for a while in my affections, but finally the lilac won, because of its fragrance (although the formation and colour of the flower of the wistaria are so beautiful it was hard to put it aside). But one cannot resist the heady sweet perfume of the lilac, coming as it does in early summer, with the promise (not always fulfilled) of long blue and golden days ahead; *lily-of-the-valley*: this is my favourite flower of them all! To bury one's face in a bunch of lily-of-the-valley is one of the great joys of living! *Pansies*: think of the great companionship these little flowers would engender on a lonely island! All those innocent, beautifully-decorated faces looking up at one! What could be nicer? *Roses*: choosing which variety of rose was the most difficult task of all. Finally, but with some sadness, I rejected La France, with its heady fragrance; Rosa Mundi, even though it always looks as though it had just then stepped out of a medieval tapestry – finally I settled for William Lobb. When it first comes into bloom it is a deep crimson. Slowly it turns to mauve and finally, before it dies, it is the most exquisite colour, almost a lavender grey, so that one would have enormous value from this one, beautifully-scented rose; *Romneya coulteri*: How brilliant of Nature to endow this glorious *white* poppy with a large golden eye and a blue-green leaf. At night it gently folds its petals inwards, so that it looks for all the world like a beautiful white swan whose wings are made from very finely pleated white linen.

Lady Diana Cooper

LONDON
Author and socialite

Thank you for asking me to join the game – will this do? Regale *lily*, preferably yellow; *amaryllis*, preferably white; *passion flower*; *cymbidium orchid*, preferably pink; wild *fritillaria*; *Crown Imperial* (garden); *iris* – fleur de Luce; *camellia*; *azaleas* en masse; Queen Elizabeth *roses*.

H E Sergio da Costa

UNITED NATIONS, NEW YORK CITY
Brazilian Ambassador to the United Nations

Orchid (cattlyea); *lily* (canna); *rose*; *paeony*; *tulip*; *magnolia*; *camellia*; *mimosa*; *iris*; *African daisy*.

Why did I select those particular flowers as my choices to take with me to a 'desert' island? I did not have to ponder too long before I realized:

1 I like flowers that say 'Here I am!', flowers that make their presence known, as opposed to such shy and retiring blossoms as forget-me-nots, violets and alyssum, for instance, which you have to peer at carefully before they can be seen and identified. Yes, the magnolia is very short-lived but, for me, its beauty is such that, while it lasts, it is eternity.

2 I like flowers to be decorative, to communicate with the beholder, to give enjoyment at their very sight.

3 I prefer flowers that are fragrant. Only one or two of my choices are not. Take the cattlyea, for instance – after all, it can forego fragrance, such is its beauty.

Mrs Justin Dart

LOS ANGELES
Wife of Californian industrialist

Here are my flowers, and *why*: for red and adaptability, *Indian paintbrush*; for pink and stability, *lotus*; for orange (coral) and independence, oriental *poppy*; for yellow and happiness, *buttercup* and *daffodil*; for green and originality, *zinnia*; for blue and innocence, the heavenly *Morning Glory*; for lavender and honesty, *pansy*; for white and remembrance, *lily-of-the-valley* and *narcissus*.

Lanham Deal

SEATTLE

Director of the
Seattle Symphony Orchestra

Fleur's Island, true to its name, would be made entirely of flowers. Since there would be no gardener, in fact – God forbid – no humans at all, the flowers would be exclusively wild flowers. But even wild flowers are wont to carry memories, and some of them are human.

There would be pasture *thistles*, reminiscent of a field at Great Surries and, in honour of the pasture's owner, a scattering of dent-de-lion, *dandelions*.

It would warm the hearts of former Texans if they might be remembered by a small field of *bluebonnets*, perhaps adjoining a land blanket of yellow *mustard*. On a tip of the island once struck by lightning, *fireweed* would have sprung up, not far from the pond where *water lily* leaves provide ample seats for the island's frogs. Let there be some *yucca*, at its best from dusk to dawn, to delight the night creatures.

In a woody glen, let's find some *Dutchmen's Breeches* from the Pacific Northwest, an area too infrequently visited by a painter from London. And, farther out, in the bright sunlight, there might be a sprig of *Indian paintbrush* in case that painter forgot hers.

But the island would need music. Since it is an imaginary island, an imaginary flower could meet the need. I will call it a *bisbigliando* after that whispering sound made by a harp. The blossom would resemble a Bird of Paradise but with silver threads strung between the petals by a great blue spider, to be played by the winds.

H E Jaime Zobel de Ayala

MANILA

Former Philippines Ambassador
to the Court of St James

What a refreshing and beautiful idea and how wonderful to set aside for a moment complicated business matters and think of flowers instead!

Being the tropical man that I am, I'm thinking mostly of flowers that grow in my country, but I do have reminiscences of Spain and England too, so here are the ten flowers that I would take with me to a lonely island: *rose*; *chrysanthemum*; *bougainvillea*; *poppy* (wild); *camellia*; *frangipani* (here in The Philippines, we call it Calachuchi – Frangipani is a Hawaiian name, I believe); *orchid*; *gardenia*; *wisteria*; *sampaguita* (our national flower). I have chosen these flowers for their scent, their colour and their shape.

Baroness de Courcel

PARIS
Wife of former French Ambassador
to the Court of St James

Being a lover of flowers, but not a gardener, I would not dream for a minute of taking flowers with me to a lonely island – therefore the only flowers I would take with me would be '*Les Fleurs du Mal*' – the other possibility could be to take '*Fleur*' (*Cowles*) – at least one would be sure not to be bored!

Mme Paly Deferre

MARSEILLES
Flower lover

Tulips; *daffodils*; *frutesceus*; bull finch *paeonia*; *aubretia*; *aster* (La Vahoise – blue with yellow heart); *petunia*; *verbena*; *love-in-the-mist*; *plumbago*.

Charles de Haes

GLAND, SWITZERLAND
Director-General of the World Wildlife Fund

Below are the ten flowers I should like to take to my lovely island. With the exception of the first, they are not in order of preference. I have listed an eleventh in case you think one flower might not qualify:

Fleur Cowles *rose*; *carnation*; *agapanthus*; *chincherinchee*; *bougainvillea*; *poinsettia*; *arum lily*; *protea*; *strelitzia*; *chrysanthemum*.

Olivia de Havilland

PARIS
Actress and author

Freesias; *frangipani*; *violets*; *irises*; *bluebells*; *daffodils*; *lily-of-the-valley*; *water lilies*; *paeonies*; *delphiniums*.

Mme Guy de Keller

VAUD, SWITZERLAND
Wife of Swiss Ambassador to Ireland, 1966–70

My flower island would have three hundred and sixty-four days of glorious sunshine and one of dark clouds and heavy rain. Otherwise, correct watering would take place from gentle miracle clouds assembled as necessary for the varying needs of my flower friends. I think the approach to my island would be a lane of *auratum lilies* against a background of green-black *holly* leaves and the Chilean shrub of the same colour but without the prickles. This lane would make a secret of everything to come. The secrets would unfold, first of all in a rose garden of the old-fashioned *rose* Muscosa and other large, strongly-scented gems. The rose in particular is a messenger of mysticism, its history many-splendoured. First depicted in the House of Frescoes at Knossos, Crete, in the sixteenth century BC, it eventually gave its name to the island of Rhodes. The ancient Greeks and Romans sensibly used rose petals for sensuous enjoyment: rose petal mattresses were among their luxuries. In the Middle Ages, Christians used the rose to make tightly pressed petals into rosary beads. Legends abound, too numerous for brevity. In the language of love, 'the red rose whispers of passion, the white rose speaks of love'. I would like them happily mixed.

Then, for fun, I would have a field of wild *narcissi*. The white field would be an unexpected touch on a desert island. Useless to relate the well-known story of Narcissus (whom I don't like anyway). I do love the flowers because, when the snows melt, the gods of the mountains seem to regret the sparkling white. They replace the snow with fields of narcissi, prolonging a white landscape and filling the air with the scent of Elysium.

For a game of contrasts I would have a small area of baby *myrtles* in mini-Versailles tubs. Arranged, perhaps, in the shape of a heart. Everyone knows the myrtle tree, its symmetrical look, the story of its importance to the Greeks and Romans and, in our times, the tradition of including a sprig of myrtle in wedding bouquets. The baby myrtle is not so well known. Ideally a perfect ball of small dark green leaves on a short tree trunk, it produces flowers like tiny, spicy white feathers. Legend claims that the miniature was first cultivated by George Washington and it can now be seen in the mini-topiary garden of Mrs Paul Mellon.

In the middle of the baby myrtle heart, I might have an enormous *Rhododendron griffithianum*. This rhododendron of Sikkim is as rare as it is beautiful. The leaves are shiny green on top, bronze below, and the enormous bell flowers are pure white with a delicate, spicy scent. Well-known in Tibet, this rhododendron was revealed to the Western world through the drawings of J. D. Hooker in 1849. It flourishes in the garden of Mr Henry McIlhenny in Ireland's County Donegal where unusual flowers thrive far from their native habitat. He has his own magic garden in reality.

Somewhere there would have to be a mass of *Hydrangea macrophylla* (blue wave). I love this hydrangea for its shape, its colour and because, when dried, it becomes an elusive pale blue-green. It is a native of Japan where the young leaves are used for making tea. They are also dried to be used in the washing of images on the Buddha's birthday. My island would have some Japanese statuary so the leaves might be useful.

Of course there would have to be giant *elm* trees so that a huge carpet of *bluebells* would appear in the spring – the sky brought down to earth for a few sublime weeks.

Mady de la Giraudière

PARIS
Primitive painter

Merci de penser à moi pour ce choix très difficile!!! Voici mes fleurs préférés – hélas en français.

Une marguerite, des bleuets, des coquelicots (le drapeau français, n'est-ce pas?!), boutons d'or, pied d'alouettes, tulipe noire, boule de neige, livoine rose, zinias, campanules.

En fait, j'aime les dix fleurs qui me permettent de faire un bouquet où figureront touts les couleurs! Il ya a surtout des fleurs des champs que je préfére aux autres car je trouve que leur existence tient d'un miracle de Dieu puisque personne ne les arrose, ou entretient. J'aime leur coté sauvage!

Baron Philippe de Rothschild

PAULLIAC, FRANCE
Grower of the world's finest wines

Question: choose the ten flowers you would like to take to a lonely island (assuming *anything* would grow there). There are many ways of approaching the problem. My choice could really be classified under different headings, i.e.: (1) by seasons from spring through to winter; (2) flowers as flowers and flowering shrubs; (3) outdoor flowers and indoor flowers; (4) flowers for their fragrance and flowers for their looks; (5) in the house – cut flowers for vases and flowers grown in a pot.

Everything considered, my preference cannot be limited to ten. Minimum number – thirteen. (I was born on a 13th.) They are as follows: an invisible flower: that of the *vine*, for what it promises; in the house: flowers grown in pots – *tuberose, stephanotis, jasmine, gardenia, fuchsia, orchid* (one species only, commonly known in French as Sabot de Venus); shrubs: *camellias, choisias, cotoneasters*; in a bed (not mine): *iris*; cut flowers: *arum lilies, freesias.*

H E Carlos Ortiz de Rozas

ROME
Diplomat

To an imaginary island I would take ten flowers selected not because of their beauty, scent or other inherent qualities, but rather for what they represent in our own conventional language. They are, in the following order:

The *rose* (love), *acacia* (friendship), *water willow* (freedom), *olive* (peace), *daffodil* (regard), *mimosa* (sensitivity), *turnip* (charity), *amaryllis* (beauty), yellow *jasmine* (elegance and grace) and the *flowering almond* (hope).

If I were permitted to add another to the established limit of ten flowers, I would include the lemon to put some 'zest' into all the previously-mentioned attributes which I would like to see growing in that marvellous island of yours and everywhere else in the world.

Nancy Dickerson

WASHINGTON, DC
Political writer and television commentator

Of course I'll play a game – most anything you want – and I'm delighted to play your flower game. It's already given me pleasure just to think about all the beautiful flowers I've seen and, remembering them, to try to be judicious. It's not easy to limit myself to ten, but I trust you won't publish in 'flower language' so those left out won't be hurt: *forsythia*; *daffodil*; *lily-of-the-valley*; *geranium*; *chrysanthemum*; *anemone*; *cherry blossom*; red *poppy*; *dogwood*; *snowdrop* (and a *rose*, if done by Fleur).

Enrico Donati

NEW YORK CITY
Painter

If I leave for an island to be alone I will think about two things. One is food and the other is dream. I am not going to take ten flowers; I am going to take two flowers. One will be a *cauliflower* (for food); the other a *poppy*, which will make me dream and think I am in paradise. As I will never get to paradise because I am not good enough, at least the poppy will give me a feeling of dreamland.

The colour will be red because it means love forever. The cauliflower colour is the colour of spaghetti, and it is not because of the colour that I love them both. If I were on a deserted island, I certainly would not try to fish because I wouldn't be able to un-hook the fish, and so I would end up starving. That is why I need the cauliflower.

Hebe Dorsey

PARIS
Fashion columnist, social commentator,
International Herald Tribune

Frankly and honestly, I love flowers:

Orchids – trees of pink or white orchids because orchids are like caviar. If you have to have them, splurge and never, never take one stem at a time. Again, I only like them in countries where they are a luxury. In Colombia, where even funeral wreaths are made of orchids, I'd switch to paper flowers.

I like *roses*, but only the garden variety – which come in all different and fat shapes, fall all over a vase and still smell of the garden. The only exceptions are long-stemmed pink roses – never fewer than twenty-five and sent by a lover. Otherwise, forget it.

Daisies – because they are fresh and innocent; I only like the white ones which have a perkiness that's quite appealing. I also like them because they have lots of pretty green leaves around them which makes them look opulent, despite a modest origin.

Tulips – I adore, especially pink or white ones. Hate the reds, yellows and blacks and hate mixtures. Tulips need nothing, except a clean square crystal vase. They have a life all their own and do exactly as they please, which makes them most interesting. They also last very well.

Azaleas – because of their many nuances, but I don't like them in flower pots where even the lushest ones have a slightly 'concierge' look about them. Azaleas should be seen in gardens, as in upstate New York, where their gigantic and colourful masses are quite a joy to behold.

Forsythia – in Paris, forsythia is the first sign of spring. Although I'm not crazy about yellow flowers, the greatest pleasure I get from spring comes from the early-blooming forsythia. I always had lots of it in my garden and, even now, on my balcony because forsythia means hope.

Lilac – I like them in December, white and in big masses because this means, again, the height of luxury. Or I like to see big masses of them in the garden in June. I like both the simple and the double flower but, somehow, I don't like to pick it. If in season, I prefer to see it outside.

Magnolia – another favourite because of its magnificent wax-like flowers. I prefer the pale ones but also liked the arrangement I had in a Maisons Laffite garden of two magnolia trees close to each other and bearing flowers of two different shades of pink. I also learned not to pick magnolia branches; they are clumsy and stiff and do not last.

Asters – because they mix so well with other summer flowers and have such a wide variety of colours. They also look as good in a garden as in a vase.

Paeonies – I learned to love them in England where we stopped at a bed-and-breakfast paeony farm years ago. The landlady had a unique way of arranging lovely fresh paeonies in simple white vases which I found quite enchanting. I have loved them ever since.

Kirk Douglas

BEVERLY HILLS
Actor and producer

My most favourite flower is the white *lilac*, the only pleasant memory I have from my childhood in the poor district of Amsterdam, New York. My second choice is *tulip*, any colour. Then: *chrysanthemums* (any colour); *bougainvilleas*; *forget-me-nots*; *daisies*; *orchids* (small ones on long stems, not the horrid, large, purple ones!).

Mrs Lewis Douglas

NEW YORK CITY
Widow of US Ambassador
to the Court of St James, 1947–50

You asked me, dear Fleur, what flowers mean to me. How can anyone describe the sky? Living, growing beauty that goes on and on – this flowers mean to me. And this is why my husband and I so loved the wild flowers of Arizona: *desert delphinium* – brilliant blue; *owl's clover*; *desert poppies* – bright orange; *desert verbena*; *prickly poppies*, dead white; *shasta flowers*; *prickly pear blooms*, every bright colour.

Betsy Drake

LONDON
Actress and writer

I'd love to play your flower game, despite the sad fact that I am terrible at flower names even though I remember their faces.

Roses – particularly yellow, yellow-orange, deep pink, sweet-smelling; big, white, *African daisies*; *rhododendron* – the kind I saw in Kew Gardens last spring; tall *tulips*, any colour – the white and pale yellow that I grew in Beverly Hills were willowy, reminding me of dancers. The big fat ones that I see in London are amazing and I'd want to take them too; *English primulas*, in all colours – I have them in pots on a ledge outside my kitchen window and they're blooming right now; *iris* – royal blue velvet with yellow in the centre; *Japanese poppies*, bright red-orange, yellow-orange in particular; *anemone* – I see many colours in my mind's eye; *ginger* – it blooms in California in August and fills the house with perfume; last but not least, the lovely flower that surprises me every August and September, the belladona lily – *Amaryllis belladonna* – the one that grows in my garden is lilac colour with a sweet smell, three feet high and called 'multiflora rosea' – large bulbs, genus: Brunsvigia, family: Amaryllidaceae.

Etienne Dreyfous

PARIS

Director-General of AIR FRANCE

On a desert island she would always be round the corner and I would wish:

A *hibiscus*, for her to tell me that she is free; a *marguerite*, for her to know that she loves me; a *lotus*, so that she may show it; a *snowdrop*, to chase the winter away; a *crocus*, to embrace her feet; a *gardenia*, to crown my queen; a *rose*, to perfume the morning; a *jasmine*, to perfume the evening; a *frangipani*, ready to welcome a guest; a *carnation*, and why not . . . for me!

Paul Dufau

LE LAUSSOU, FRANCE

Late painter whose work I collected

Le *lilas*; la *pervenche*; l'*aubepine*; la *tulipe*; la *rose*; la *violette*; le *jasmin*; la *lavande*; la *marguerite*; le *coquelicot*.

Irene Dunne

LOS ANGELES
Actress

Wherever I am I must have a rose garden. Here are some of my favourites:

Success, Bewitched, Colour Magic, Peace, First Prize, Mr Lincoln, King's Ransom, Kentucky Derby, Eiffel Tower, Pascali.

If there is a rose named Fleur, I am sure it is beautiful and I would substitute one of these for it.

Gerald Durrell

JERSEY, CHANNEL ISLANDS
Author and Chairman
of the Jersey Wildlife Trust

Mesembryanthemum (we have a small purply-magenta one here – a sort of Mexican pink which is terribly pretty); *chrysanthemum* (bronze and yellow); *freesia*; *flax*; *scarlet pimpernel*; *rose* (the old-fashioned floppy kind which smell like Victorian ladies); flower of the *olive tree*; *sea lily*; *crocus*; pink *magnolia*.

Sylvia Earle

OAKLAND, CALIFORNIA
Marine biologist

The list of ten is *almost* an arbitrary selection. It could so easily, and justifiably, include cattails and blue-eyed grass, bluettes, physalia, galivin, gentian, wood rush and lady slippers. It should have croomia for special, wonderful visions that this small flower brings to mind of a time before recent ice ages when forests were arranged in rather considerably different patterns than is evident in the twentieth century. It would not be my idea of 'living' to be without manzanita and diogenes lantern, or the jade-like flowers of grape vines (and their ultimate products!). I would, if I could, also take a plant I have seen only once – the Chilean copihue, a flower that to me is almost a mystical symbol of the vulnerability of living things in this era of extraordinary change. If I could, I would take *all* of the proteas along – I would surround myself with desert plants, and those of rain forests, of high mountains, and open plains, to have close at hand plants whose time line precedes our own by thousands or millions of years – and whose time may pass as we watch (except, maybe, on your island!).

I finally assembled a whimsical collection that assumes a magic world where you can have your plants without having to eat them too: *daffodil* – maybe it is because I spent my childhood in New Jersey (where spring never came soon enough to suit me and the appearance of daffodils was a sure sign that I would soon have shoe-less freedom outside) that these flowers have a special place in my mind and heart. In their presence, like slipping into a time machine, I feel nine years old. Actually, it is a toss-up between daffodils and blue iris. I can't imagine one without the other somewhere nearby; *zephyr lily* – like daffodils, the wild lilies mean spring to me but, unlike daffodils, they also convey a sense of wildness that does wonderful things to my pulse; *duckweed* – lemna blossoms I admire as fragile-looking forms that consist mostly of unadorned essentials, the epitome of simplicity. Although most of my aquatic inclinations are marine, I do love ponds and all the good things that live there that don't thrive in a salty atmosphere. Since duckweed requires a still-water/fresh-water habitat, maybe I could sneak a few other good green things in around the edges that share the need for a swamp . . . pitcher plants? A few sundews? Some sedges?

Welwitchia – impossible! That's what I thought when I first learned about this incredible Southern African citizen with its two long leaves unlike those produced by anyone else alive. Such individuality I would like to have nearby to admire and wonder at, and since I suspect that a fair chunk of desert would have to come along to surround the welwitchia and keep it in context, alive and well, perhaps again, I could count on a few associates – beetles and lizards and others that seem capable of easily doing what I cannot: surviving with only now-and-then access to water; *baobab* – baobab blossoms are beautiful in their own right and they do, moreover, grow on baobab trees that in turn host a microcosm that could keep me entertained for several lifetimes, or perhaps forever; *willow* – I am not particular about which willow, just some kind with furry catkins and the stream or swamp or meadow or tundra that would, I hope, necessarily be attached; *pear* – or peach or apple or apricot or cherry. But if I *had* to choose one of these, it would be a seckle pear, white, fragile, fragrant, with a bee hovering nearby.

Sea oats – I should be practical and choose one of the equally beautiful grass flowers that would also yield corn muffins, ultimately, or oatmeal or bread. One of my early lists consisted of *just* grasses – sweet vernal, rattlesnake, pampas, spartina – and here I go again, reconsidering the possibilities . . . If human beings were characteristically three inches high, the awesome beauty of grass flowers would not go unnoticed. Luckily for me, one of my professors and friends, Hugo Blomquist, had a passion for grasses that he shared readily. Holding a hand lens between his eye and the blossom, 'Bloomie' described what he saw, as if he were, in fact, three inches high, standing next to silver bristles, brilliant yellow pollen sacs, arching bracts, incredible feathery structures. Sea oats are lovely in their own right, but also as a way of putting down roots in fine places. To me they reflect the essence of a sea coast.

Dandelion – as a child, I used to wonder at the sanity of adults who spent huge amounts of time and money to eradicate what to me seemed to be a totally beguiling, beautiful, useful, hardy, benign, lovely creation, from shimmering silver puffs at the end of summer to the hauntingly symmetrical discs of petals in early spring. As an adult, I still wonder at the war waged on dandelions in lawns and gardens but smile, recognizing the hardy nature of a plant that manages not only to survive – but to thrive – in old fields, in the cracks in sidewalks, in wild places (and tame), apparently indifferent to the peculiar ways – and tastes – of mankind; *thalassia* – as with grasses, I put together one 'list of ten' of just flowering plants in the sea. I would be content to be surrounded by these, of course, and have, and will – as much as I am able – during my time on the planet. Of the fifty or so 'sea-grasses,' it isn't easy to select one (or even *ten* of the fifty). Should I leave behind the delicate deepest-growing species, halophila baillonis? How could there not be poseidonia? or syringodium? Or the 'eel grass' that I knew as a child in bays along the Atlantic coast? I suppose, if really pressed to take one and only one, I would choose Thalassia – turtle grass – for a combination of practical and sentimental reasons. Among the most productive plants on earth, the subsea meadows of Thalassia provide food and shelter for some of my favourite things: shrimp, crabs, urchins, fish, octopuses. The beauty of the blossoms is also much to my liking: whenever I find the seldom-seen starbursts of translucent green and pink, I react with irrational, total delight.

Viscount Eccles

LONDON
UK Minister of the Arts, 1970–73

I would take ten kinds of *rose*.

Douglas Fairbanks Jr

PALM BEACH
Actor, writer and producer

The dark red (or Harvard red) *carnation*, as I have worn one in my button-hole actually since I have had a button-hole; the *rose*, and don't forget we had a bed of Fleur Cowles planted at The Boltons and they were beautiful – two other lovely varieties that we had in the garden were Cardinal Richelieu and Roger Lamblin; the *tulip*, for their symmetry and line, and I particularly like them when they go off in all directions; the hybrid *hibiscus*, which we are growing here, that lasts for three days off the bush – they are in gaudy, wonderful colours, the size of a plate, and very strong; the *hollyhock*, for sentiment and childhood memories; the *tuberose*, for pure sensual scent delight; *pansies*, for their smiling faces; the *amaryllis*, again for purity of line; the *lily-of-the-valley*, for delicacy and scent; the *ranunculus*, for the quality of its petal.

If I could go on, I would certainly include the anemone, because I feel the colours are so wonderful. Also, the tiger lily, which in addition to having an exquisite scent, seems to incorporate everything: beauty, colour, delicacy and it is long-lasting.

Temple Fielding

MALLORCA
Editor, *Fielding Guides*

In replying to your fun-filled request, here are the ten flowers which I love the most: Harvard red dwarf *carnations* for topcoat bouton-nières; *jasmine*; *agapanthus*; *calceolaria*; *lily-of-the-valley*; yellow *roses*; *hyacinths*; *night blooming cereus*; *water lily*; *Judas trees*. Among my pet hates are: Birds of Paradise; gladioli; zinnias.

Joan Fontaine

NEW YORK CITY
Actress

Tuberose; *hyacinth*; *narcissus daffodil*; *tulip*; *daphne*; *lilac*; *wisteria*; *delphinium*; *violet*; *rose*.

Dame Margot Fonteyn

LONDON AND PANAMA
Prima ballerina

Yes, I would be delighted to play the flower game and the ten flowers I have chosen are: *paeonies*; *fuchsias*; *freesias*; *gardenias*; *wisteria*; *camellias*; *magnolia*; white *lilacs*; *jonquils*; *roses*.

Bryan Forbes

WENTWORTH, SURREY

Film director and producer

My wife Nanette Newman seems to have stolen most of my thunder, as well as my blooms so, assuming we are both marooned on separate islands, I would choose *camellias*, hoping to grow them into a tree strong enough eventually to make me a raft, on which I could travel across water to find Nanette again!

I would start with *roses*, something strong and resistant like Queen Elizabeth and maybe Papa Meilland because of its overpowering scent. I like *bluebells*, because they evoke childhood memories, as do primulas. Then I would want sweet smelling *night stocks* to waft me to my lonely island bed. *Honeysuckle* I would want to twine round the door of my driftwood shack on the beach and, emulating Nanette, I would opt for wild *poppies* scattered amongst alien *corn*. Then, to remind me of the seasons I would plant *freesia* and *daffodils* because, in Wordsworth's words, I am sure I would spend many hours 'wandering lonely as a cloud'.

There you are – a purely romantic list – so please hurry and find me the island because I long to get away from the rat race.

Christina Foyle

LONDON

Foyle's Bookshop

I should love to play the flower game with you, especially as my garden is my greatest delight. Most of all I love scented flowers and that is why these are great favourites: *daphne*; *datura*; *tobacco* – nicotiana; mock orange – *philadelphus*; old-fashioned *roses*; *lily-of-the-valley*. Also: convolvulus – *Morning Glory*, because it is the flower that you always see in charming pictures of fairies and seems to be the favourite flower in the world of fantasy; *cyclamen*, because it is practically the first flower to appear after the winter; I love the *bluebells* in my wood, and I am very fond of *nasturtiums* because they were my father's favourite flower and they remind me very much of him.

Massimo Freccia

LONDON
Symphony conductor

As an aesthete I firstly thought of a *Bird of Paradise* (strelitzia), of the elegant *Aztec lily*, of the showy *Hindu lotus* and the *Japanese snowball*. If I overlook the spirit and indulge in more carnal pleasure, the *gardenia* and *lily-of-the-valley* would be my choice.

But while immersed in these spiritual and sensual dreams, my Florentine down-to-earth sense of reality compels me not to overlook certain flowers, the property of which I think most necessary for my survival: *valerian* – anti-neurotic and sedative; *Bouncing Bet* – anti-gout and rheumatism; *foxglove* – cartiotonic; *angels' trumpets* – which will provide me with a heavenly band to conduct on the Day of Resurrection.

But Fleur . . . no flower can grow without you!!!

Janet Gaynor

PALM SPRINGS, CALIFORNIA
Film actress turned painter

Here are my ten – as you can see, they are all simple garden flowers, the ones I love to paint: *petunia*; *nasturtium*; *hibiscus*; *Iceland poppy*; *rose*; *cosmos*; *hydrangea*; *delphinium*; *hollyhock*; *oleander*.

Françoise Gilot-Salk

SAN DIEGO, CALIFORNIA
Author and wife of Jonas Salk,
pioneer of polio vaccine

What a lovely idea: to have peace at last in a 'desert' island with cliffs quite steep, I hope, except for a beach at the mouth of a river that I would follow higher and higher to the heart of the island. There the fresh water would fall from up above into a pool in the shape of a shell, among polished rocks.

There would be *water lilies* of course (my first choice) and, freely growing on the banks, *asphodels, columbines, foxgloves, hellebore, snowdrops, tuberoses* and *violets*.

I would swim in the emerald pool and afterwards, sitting on a rock, would braid a crown of *passion flowers*; then to rest and sleep under the shade of a dangerous *datura* that would induce . . . a dream, where my fancy would introduce me to another desert island where I could choose ten other flowers . . . etc., ad infinitum.

Mrs Thayer Gilpatric

NEW YORK CITY
Socialite

My favourite flowers are: Talisman *rose*; *pansy*; *lily-of-the-valley*; *freesia*; *sweet pea*; *coreopsis*; *lupin*; *cornflower*; double *petunia*; *Shasta daisy*.

Mrs William Goetze

SAN ANSELMO, CALIFORNIA
Sister of the author

My problem is choosing ten favourites – I have so many – but I've narrowed down a list of ten: *lily-of-the-valley*; *rose* (red, white, orange); *tulip*; *lilac*; *marigold* (large and odourless); *hyacinth*; *violet*; *daisy*; *orange blossom*; *daphne*.

54

DAR ES SALAAM
Anthropologist and author

I have had a fascinating time going through flowers in my mind. The first six flowers were very easy to choose – but the last four were much harder. Not because it is difficult to think of four flowers one loves, but because it is difficult to reject others.

The *rose* has to come first – because of the scent, the colour, the myriad associations in one's own life and in literature. Should I choose which rose? I cannot, because I do not know their names. There is a dark, dark red rose, almost black, which is so exquisite when just beginning to open, especially in a garden with dew drops. And a fantastic dark yellow one with the most fabulous scent.

The wild *violet*, because it is shy and hidden, and smells glorious, and takes me straight back into my childhood.

Lily-of-the-valley, because the scent is probably my favourite.

Then three together, because they promise spring and hope and also take me back to days long past: first the *snowdrop*. I so well remember searching for the first snowdrop to open and being so amazed that it can flower when it is still so cold. Then the *crocus*. Warmer days now, orange and mauve spikes pushing out of the ground in secret, hidden places. And the *primrose*. The countryside, blankets of primroses, along the roads, the railways.

Then come the *lilac*, those great luscious blooms with their glorious scent. And the shy *honeysuckle*, with such a delicate, wild fragrance.

But I don't think I can choose the last two because it's too unfair on all the others. The arum lily (supposed to be a reminder of death, but not for me! – just mysticism and the sun at Easter shining through the stained glass windows). Water lilies, almost like magic flowers as they float on the water amidst the flat, frog rafts of their leaves. Poppies in the gold of the stubble fields with the bright blue summer sky and the skylarks. The exotic richness of the laburnum. The dancing gold of the daffodil and the misty blue carpet of the bluebells in the cool shade of the woods. The jacaranda – bluebell-blue against the dark rain clouds in Africa. The exotic flame trees in flower. The fragrance of the acacia in bloom, pale downy yellow softening the harshness of the fearsome thorns. And what of the cowslip and the harebell, the chrysanthemum, the sunflower?

Cary Grant

LOS ANGELES
Actor

My selections, probably listed in the favour with which I regard them since they popped to mind in the following order: *pansies* – all types, all colours; *lilacs* – lavender and/or white; *bluebells*; *lily-of-the-valley*; *daisies* – not the small field daisy but the larger, single-petalled variety; *sweet peas* Lathyrus odoratus; *roses*; *violets*; *cornflowers* – blue; *jasmine*.

Though how could you limit me, or anyone, to a list of only ten? I long to add primroses, mimosa, frangipani, carnations, fuchsias . . . oh, I could go on for hours.

Dulcie Gray

AMERSHAM, BUCKINGHAMSHIRE
Actress, author

The ten flowers I would like to take with me are:
Flame of the forest – because the flowers are a magnificent orange-red that would cheer me up if I were feeling gloomy, and they grow on trees, which would give shade; wild *violet, primrose* and *cowslip* – to remind me of the England I knew as a child, when all these flowers were common in the countryside; white *roses* – because they were the first flowers my husband, Michael Denison, gave me.

Paeonies – because they are lush and fat and beautiful and were much painted in the seventeenth century by painters of the School of Utrecht to which Maria Merian's father and stepfather belonged. She gathered the various ingredients for them, including butterflies, lizards, ladybirds, etc., and in so doing noticed that an egg which became a caterpillar became a chrysalis and then a butterfly. She was the first person in Europe to be believed on the subject of metamorphosis.

Buddleia – which attracts several species of butterfly; *magnolia* – the big white ones; *Canterbury bells* (the old-fashioned kind); scarlet garden *poppies*.

HRH Prince Michel of Greece

PARIS

Unfortunately I am not a botanist but I would definitely pick up three flowers which can be transplanted anywhere and could grow in any climate: Marina, my wife: Alexandra and Olga, my two daughters.

René Gruau

CANNES
Painter

My very favourite flowers are: *gardenia* and *magnolia*, followed by *jasmine* and *tuberose*. I love their perfume but I would give gardenia the capital G as it is a real passion for me, a sort of physical, sensual feeling – almost exaggerated.

Lindy Guinness
(Marchioness of Dufferin and Avon)

LONDON
Painter

Flowers have been an endless inspiration for my painting. To discover and understand the idiosyncrasies of plants, especially their sense of individuality and life rather than the correct botanical analysis, has been my concern. I list ten flowers that I have a special relationship with; they all have been grown either in my garden in London or the one in Ireland.

Magnolia delavayi: the shape of its parchment-coloured petals is a mixture of a medicinal spoon or an angry cobra. Our tree is thirty feet high, its grand, imposing leaves radiate outwards, sculptural and erect.

Helleborus niger: the plant that I paint grows in London. I'm fascinated by its camouflage that does not quite work. These strange, green-white flowers have a mystical quality, shining in the darkest days of winter. The leaves are so complex and are moved by the wind in slow staccato rhythms.

Datura sanguinea: this exotic, hot-looking plant grows in great profusion in our greenhouse at Clandeboye. The fleshy leaves and erotic hairy pods hang from fast growing stalks. Everything is heady and scented and hot; the orange-chrome-yellow trumpet flowers belong to the Mediterranean and further east.

Iris germanica: Monet understood about the iris – so did the painters in China and Japan. Their forms are a mixture of strict, ordered leaves contrasting with the flowers that open and offer unimaginable beauty.

Paeonia off. rubra plena: in the evening light of June I have often painted the tree paeony in London – its magenta-red flowers held against the green leaves always recalls the particular colour relationships in a Matthew Smith. He understood in the fullest and most painterly fashion these aristocratic and sometimes overwhelming plants.

Rose, Park Director Riggers: a beautiful semi-single form which grows on an old wall in Ireland, and gives such joy in late September. Its dark ruby red petals have the perfection that was so admired by Persian miniaturists. Their translucent quality holds silently the evening light. They are impossibly difficult to paint.

Lily candiocrinum giganteum: after many patient years of waiting I flowered this six-foot lily and felt a prayer had been answered. A most wondrous sight! The flowers are held out, angled towards the centre, white and scented. I stood painting it, looking up into the flowers. I failed dismally to say what I felt in the painting, but I will never forget the experience.

Lily (Golden Splendour): I painted it over three days, watching it from the bud stage until its full flowering. How humble and simple it looked on its first day and then, on opening, what wild and glorious a celebration to summer – its golden speckled flowers obsessed me for hours.

Clematis (Ville de Lyon): a most lovely plant – its bruised magenta – red against slighty blue – tinged leaves twine and intertwine with a passion flower in a jumble of confusion in our cool greenhouse, where I painted them this summer.

Rhododendron lyndlii: this scented, waxy-white rhododendron grows in a wooded glade guarded from the winds by an old yew. Its flowers shine like torches against the green, and its scent pervades our water garden. Painting it this summer I was brought back to earth by the midges!

Lady Henderson

WASHINGTON, DC
Wife of UK Ambassador
to the United States

I love the flowers in my cottage garden at Combe more than the ones in the various Embassy gardens we have had – so my choice comes from there. But I must confess that I really love arranging flowers and having flowers in my room. Nicko accuses me – and he is right – of looking at a garden to see what I will pick.

I hope there will be a mug or a scooped out coconut on the 'desert' island as I would like to see growing, and be able to pick, a small bunch of: *pansies* – I love their faces and their deep maroon and purple colours; *aquilegias* – they are so fragile and decorative; they look wild and yet are not wild.

Now, the next four you may say are not flowers, but I must have them with me. I mix them in my bunches of flowers and I need their scent: *basil*, *thyme*, *lavender* and *mint*. I would bring *roses* of course, but the old-fashioned ones: Fantin-Latour, which is really like 'R' for rose and which frames my cottage window. It would be accompanied by my favourite climber – the pale, almost holy, *passion flower*, which some Greek peasants call The Virgin. *Rosa Mundi* would come too, because our family have a stripe complex and there is no prettier rose. And finally, I would take the *crested moss rose*, which brings back fairy tale memories and must have been the rose that grew around Sleeping Beauty.

Joanne Herring

HOUSTON
Hostess and television personality

Rubrum lily; *paeony*; *rhododendron*; *camellia*; *night blooming jasmine*; *moonflower*; *hibiscus*; *passion flower*; *rose* (Peace).

David Hicks

LONDON
Interior designer, author

Old-fashioned *rose*; *jasmine*; *Magnolia grandiflora*; *datura*; *tuberose*; *lily*; *hellebore*; *paeony*; *hyacinth*; *Iris stylosa*.

Lady Holland

EASTLEACH, GLOUCESTERSHIRE
Socialite

My 'desert' island flowers would all be chosen to give me joy in the evening and· at night, when dusk and darkness bring fear and loneliness. Therefore they are all in shades of cream and white to glow in the half-light and are all strongly scented to enchant the night.

Colianthes tuberosa (the Chinese in Java use the flowers to make vegetable soup – I am sure it is delicious!); *Stephanotis floribunda*; *Jasminium officinale*; *syringa*: I should build an arbour with the foregoing three, as they are all climbers, and sit beneath it.

Pamianthe peruviana – because in real life it needs a near-wizard of a gardener to make it grow – even in the most exotic greenhouse! *Illicium anisatum* – in Japan the bark is burned as incense round Buddhist temples, so one would have a fire as well; *Lilium candidum* (the Madonna lily) – to symbolize my Christian faith; *Gardenia jasminoides* – to wear in my hair in case one were rescued in a hurry – it would make it look a little less tatty!; *Narcissus poeticus* (the 'pheasant's eye') – to make me thankful I was *not* on a cold wet pheasant shoot in England! *Datura suaveolens* – in case I wished to commit suicide: if you sleep beneath it the erotic dreams are such as kill you with delight (cf the death of the princess in Meyerbeer's opera *L'Africaine*) – and what a way to go!

Lord Home of the Hirsel

COLDSTREAM, BERWICKSHIRE
UK Prime Minister, 1963–4

Here are my ten flowers: the *rose*; the *paeony*; the *azalea*; the *primrose*; the *daffodil*; the *anemone*; the *rhododendron*; the *philadelphus*; the *lilac*; the *clematis*.

Roger Horchow

DALLAS
Catalogue-King

Red *roses*, long stem; blue *hyacinths*; yellow *jonquils*; blue *lilacs*; blue *wisteria*; blue *hydrangeas*; *pansies*; *forsythia*; yellow *orchid*; *zinnias* – all colours.

Beverley Jackson

SANTA BARBARA, CALIFORNIA
Socialite, commentator

I love all flowers so it would be difficult to narrow to ten – but I will. The thinking behind my choices – they fall, quite automatically, into categories – of what I feel, smell, see and, oh yes, remember – of what I remember . . .

For fragrance I would have to have:

Narcissus – all the beauty of daffodils scaled down to tiny size to compensate for their great gift, magnificent perfume; *sweet peas* – gentle colour, amusing shape, lovely fragrance, gentle and yet so sturdy on the stem, the perfect mixer of the garden (could you say the Mme Recamier of the floral world?); *roses* – lovely of texture, colour, fragrance and so nostalgic – the shell-pink wonders that wound over the walls of my childhood home, the discovery of twelve red roses deep in waxy green tissue paper in a great white box bringing messages of love, the old wild rose on woody, thorny stem encountered unexpectedly in an abandoned world: roses – a perfection in our world where perfection is an endangered species;

tuberoses – fragrance, oh yes, fragrance! The ultimate! The Concorde soaring past the speed of sound, the largest wave crashing on the whitest sand beach, the dazzle of the most perfectly cut diamond, the splendour of a Chinese red lacquer room – all the impact of these from one breath of this Grand Opera of fragrance!

For colour:

Bougainvillea – the deep magenta, purple and orange of warm days in Mexico, Spain, the south of France, Rapallo and Portofino, my own beautiful Santa Barbara where bougainvillea grows luxuriantly into massive walls of colour, not spidery trails; *Iceland poppies* – sinfully vibrant colours with lovely Fortuny-pleated petals radiating from the sundish centres; *pansies* – the yellow of the Sun Gods, the purple of Kings, those enchanting fragrant little floral people!; *sunflowers* – so rightfully named – the gold from the sun, the gold from the earth, the soldier's stance, sentinels of colour.

And, just because I love them best:

Daffodils – the memory of discovery as a four-year-old, the words 'A host of golden daffodils' right there in a green meadow. Visually, what colour brings more sense of brightness than yellow? The reflection of the sun, of gold, all richness and warmth – the posture of the daffodil, so upright, so noble and yet so gently fluted. Flowering *peach blossoms* – all feminity and frivolity in velvety-pink clusters, and what is more magical than to be caught in a wind shower of fragrant peach blossom petals?

The Raj Mata of Jaipur

INDIA

Socialite, politician

Jasmine – in India we call it Radh ki Rani, which means Queen of the Night. I love the smell of jasmine, especially as night falls and the breeze brings the sweet scent of the flower into the home; *rose* – nothing can beat the rose for looks; *sweet peas* – I love them; *arum lilies*; *narcissi*; *paeonies*; *lotus*; *orchids*; *lily-of-the-valley*; *fuchsias*.

Margaret Jay

LONDON
Television commentator

I have listed my favourite flowers which, I am afraid, are not based on any great horticultural or aesthetic distinction, but more on my enjoyment of our two gardens in London and Ireland. They are:

White *narcissus*; *rhododendrons*; climbing *roses*, especially Albertine; *iris*; *lilac*; wild *geranium*; *agapanthus lily*; *paeony*; *wood anemone*; white or gold double *chrysanthemum*.

Mrs Henry Clyde Johnson

BLOOMFIELD HILLS, MICHIGAN
Socialite

My ten favourite flowers to take to a lonely island?

Of course, the *rose* – like those you grow in your garden, luxuriously around the trunks of trees, the loveliest I have ever seen; the *lilac* – when I am far from home and see lilacs blooming, I have a mad compulsion to rush home to see our own tall, old bushes, overgrown with knotted limbs loaded with blooms, lavenders, deep purples, white; the *trillium* – yes, even over the crocus and the violet; *daffodils* by the thousands; an unending bed of *periwinkle*, carpetlike; *phlox* for its faithful perennialness, bursting in huge clumps of colour when other colour has faded; and, since it is a lonely island, large things growing with abandon: *dogwood*; *forsythia*, huge and unclipped; wild *rhododendrons*, as they grow on our South-eastern coast and in Pennsylvania; great flowering trees without symmetry, an American Beauty *malus*, for instance.

How provocative you are! Such a simple concept and yet, your lonely island will become an enchanted island. *Your* flowers, no doubt, will convert to panaceas, wine and nectar, and food for the soul.

Mrs Lyndon B Johnson

STONEWALL, TEXAS
Widow of US President, 1963–9

Since I am an intensely practical person, I would choose flowers which give the most results for the least work; *zinnias* and *marigolds* and white *daisies* would have to be on my list of favourite flowers. In my lifetime experience, I have found them to be so hardy and they give a great profusion of colour over long weeks – I've always saluted their generosity!

And it is just not possible to omit the *rose*, in all its infinite variety. To me, it is the queen of blossoms.

Both nostalgia and the love of springtime would make me include the *daffodil* and *narcissus*. In the days of my childhood in deep East Texas, the front yard of our 'Brick House' was filled with them. They were a sign that spring had returned with all its new hope and excitement. *Violets*, too, come to my mind from that time – I remember collecting sweet bouquets of them from beneath the branches and along the springs in the piney woods nearby.

Especially for me, I could not leave out the wild flowers that grow here on the Edwards Plateau of Texas. The most abundant and most loved are *bluebonnets*, *gaillardia* (Indian paintbrush or firewheel) and *coreopsis*. One can see entire pastures of them and sometimes glorious 'Persian carpets' of them all together in April and May if the Lord sends rain.

Kenneth Kendall

LONDON
BBC newscaster

What a difficult choice to make! My final selection will give me great pleasure on that 'desert' island but I know I shall be full of regrets at what I've left out. There's no significance in the order of my choice. Some have particular associations but all are there because, quite simply, I like them!

Viola (Heartsease) – not only is this a very delightful, spreading flower, but it is thought by some to have beneficial properties for the heart; *passion flower* – I like its dramatic, almost vulgar colouring when in flower, preceded by its delicate buds and followed by big orange seed-pods – plenty of interest; *paeony* – a reminder of happy childhood days spent with an aunt in Devon whose garden in May and June was a riot of these big, blowsy blooms; *hibiscus* – particularly the scarlet variety, to remind me of even earlier childhood days spent in India where they grew so well; *camellia* – this would always bring to mind Cornwall, where my family originates. Not only is the flower beautifully shaped, but the glossy leaves are a delight.

Rose Super Star – just about the most popular of all roses, but I make no apology for including it! *Fuchsia* – a double red and white variety. Always at least one in my London garden; *escallonia* – to make a flowering hedge. They do well by the sea and provide another reminder of Cornwall; *aquilegia* – delicate and somehow very English; *everlasting pea* – to me much prettier than ordinary sweetpeas. It climbs beautifully and gives a mass of bloom. It too would remind me of my London garden.

Tessa Kennedy

LONDON
Interior architect

When you asked me to write down ten of my favourite flowers I thought 'how easy,' but to separate ten names when I love all flowers with a passion was a very difficult task. My head is filled with colours, scents, gardens, vases and greenhouses. Here, however, is a list. I hope the flowers I have omitted will forgive me:

Roses, but not just any rose. In fact, I hate the brittle colours of the newer ones. I love the old-fashioned double cabbage roses and tiny moss roses which flower in abundance throughout summer in one's garden and are a joy in any arrangement. Having been brought up in a Lutyens house, with a garden by Gertrude Jekyll, roses are my earliest memories.

Paeonies, the pale pink and white ones whose glorious balls of fluff remind me of my coming-out dress from Lanvin, of my youth and of their beauty; *amaryllis*, which I plant in my basement in stages so, at the first sign of spring, my house is filled with these regal double-headed lilies. White, pale pink and red for special occasions.

Double *tulips*: I love 'double' of practically any flower and mass them in all colours in the garden. For the house, I like to mass one colour in one vase; *orchids* – these are old friends and come back with more flowers every year. The leaves alone in their pots remind me of desert plants, and of the Middle East, which I'm crazy about.

Sweet peas: I grow these in my vegetable garden in all colours. They cheer up the vegetables and fill my house with English summer; *camellias*: my first encounter with a camellia was, again, at my coming-out dance. David Hicks and Tom Parr made a night club of navy blue velvet and studded the walls and ceiling with camellias. The smell was out of this world all evening.

Freesia, the double creamy-yellow or white which I adore as table decorations in profusion. They too smell deliciously; *blossoms*: the first sign of spring when the trees are in blossom (I couldn't bear to live in a climate without proper seasons); *pansies*: their delicate colourings – they are like butterflies floating in finger bowls or flowering in abundance in a perfect English garden.

Or *Gunnera* and *Rhubarb* – a perfect addition to a herbaceous border with their huge, out-of-scale leaves.

HRH Princess Michael of Kent

LONDON

My island would be a jungle, lush, damp (?), tropical and would have only white flowers against the patchwork of green. Mother Nature (Fleur – or the Goddess of all things that grow?) wooed and won, allows everything to grow . . .

A forest of: *moonflowers*: huge green-white trumpets welcoming the wanderer, their heavy smell addictive; uncontrolled high hedges of *philadelphus*: small white memories of orange blossom grown wild; tall trees of heady white *lilac*: bowing gracefully, and magically never turning brown; wild white *jasmine*: pushing and climbing, innocent faces and delicious sweet smell; proud white *lilies*: fine heads on each straight neck, veined pink and marking the careless with indelible golden dust.

Waxy *gardenia*: intoxicating petals curling the colour of parchment; white *camellias*: prim and round against shiny dark leaves, too proud to compete in this opium den of perfumes; frail *tuberoses*: stretching for the light, exotic scent reminding me of the Vienna student attic where they grew between double windows, a screen against the winter; above, from towering rocks, a waterfall of hanging *campanula*: tiny white stars; on the ground, the miniature *rose* Snow Carpet: eagerly covering every path and corner and here, in this barefoot paradise, no thorns.

If I could have another choice or, if you prefer, I adore: white paeonies: Whitsun roses as we call them in Austria, a promise of summer to come.

Mrs Betty Kenward

LONDON
Social chronicler

I will most certainly play the flower game with you! Though I am afraid my tastes are not at all exotic, with the exception of orchids and azaleas I love the really smelly flowers.

My first choice for flowers would be *orchids* (cymbidiums and vanda hybrids), *never* those big, floppy, mauve type, that kind American gentlemen will bunch one with!; secondly, *roses*, especially deep red, sweet-smelling roses that really do scent a room; then come *Madonna lilies*; *carnations* in all colours and, under that category, I would put pinks and border carnations as they smell so good; *azaleas* of every colour; *Sweet Williams*; *tuberoses*; *stocks*; *freesias*; and, lastly, French ornamental *cabbages*.

Deborah Kerr

KLOSTERS, SWITZERLAND
Film and stage actress

Here is my list – I hope it's not too corny!! But truly my feelings: *daffodils*; *pheasant's-eye narcissi*; *roses*; *sweet peas*; *lily-of-the-valley*; *paeonies*; *wisteria*; *freesias*; *forget-me-nots*; *gentian*.

Thank you for including me – I love *all* flowers (Fleurs) and it is hard to decide.

Eleanor Lambert

NEW YORK CITY
Publicist

I would want fragrant flowers on a 'desert' island and of course perennials, because what would happen if you had to spend your life there?

Tuberoses; *apple blossoms*; miniature *orchids*; Peace *roses* and any other rose except Dorothy Perkins; *violets*; Regale *lilies*; field *daisies*; *jasmine*; tuberous *begonias*; *snowdrops*; *moonflowers*.

David Lazer

NEW YORK CITY
Producer of *The Muppets*

My choice of flowers varies as I enter different rhythms; and at this stage I have a strong preference for wild flowers. Some of them are: *heather*; *lily-of-the-valley*; *buttercups*; *poppies*; *lavender*; *beach palm* (wild rose). Their beauty, abandonment and natural choreography thrill me and feed my soul.

Oh yes, then there is *honeysuckle, night blooming jasmine, bougainvillea* and the *blue flowers* I once saw in Texas.

Richard Leakey

NAIROBI
Anthropologist, author

A *rose* bush – preferably red flowers and a good scent; a *gardenia* bush; *violet* – domestic variety; an *African violet* – white; a creeping *honeysuckle* plant; a *citrus* bush; a *desert rose* from Africa; a small *stepeliad*; one of the white-flowered *African orchids*; and *African tiger lily*.

Dennis Lennon

LONDON
Architect

On this magic isle I suppose you could ask for anything. Could I, in addition to the flowers, ask for an endless supply of *yew hedges* which I could arrange in courtyards, avenues, bowers, from which I would get unexpected views of the sea and whose blessed shade I could enjoy? *Grass* has to be there, soft to my bare feet and, of course, cut and watered by magic overnight.

Then would come the flowers, simple Shakespearean ones, probably never in the Chelsea Flower show, like: *buttercups, daisies, bluebells, snowdrops, cowslips, cow parsley, primroses,* wild *roses, honeysuckle* and *apple blossom.*

I imagine them concentrated in areas so I could walk from a blue courtyard to a yellow down, a rose avenue to a honeysuckle arch at the end, with a vista of daisies dotting the sea and clouds beyond.

Cole Lesley

VAUD, SWITZERLAND
Biographer of Noel Coward

There are so many much more exotic flowers I grew to love in the tropics but I feel certain you want me to be honest, so I've searched my heart and this is a true list: *snowdrops; primroses; violets; lily-of-the-valley; tulips; lilac;* dark brown velvet *wallflowers; delphiniums,* deepest blue; *lilies,* the tall white garden ones; Albertine *roses,* from which I'd take cuttings and make them grow all over everything, everywhere.

Bernard Levin

LONDON
Author and critic

Buttercups; buttercups; buttercups; daisies; daisies; daisies; those-pink-things-over-there-in-the-corner; those-pink-things-over-there-in-the-corner; those-pink-things-over-there-in-the-corner; those-pink-things-over-there-in-the-corner.

69

Moira Lister
(Vicomtesse d'Orthez)

LONDON

Stage and screen actress

Herewith my little list – as you can see, deeply influenced by my youth in Africa. So, I love:

Protea: because they are a protected flower and no ordinary mortal is allowed to pick them – a right royal rule for a remarkable bloom; *strelitzia*: the flower that birds believe to be one of themselves. They alight upon it and thus unwittingly pollinate it, so propagating this bird-like beauty in their own image; *African violets*: because they remind me of the jungle. I soak mine in steaming water and watch them luxuriate as the hot humidity engulfs them; *Chincherinchee*: because of the excitement of receiving them from Africa at Christmas time, keeping them in the dark for a few days and then watching them opening their delicate buds to last long after Twelfth Night before they bend over and slowly fade away a good six weeks later; *Arum lilies*: because of the luxury of stopping the car when driving through the glorious Paarl Valley where they grow wild and literally filling one's arms with as many as one can carry – all for free.

Mesembryanthemums: because as a child, our great game on a very, very hot day was to find a bank covered with their thick leaves filled with water and roll all the way down the hill, squelching and cooling ourselves at the same time; *mimosa*: because it was forbidden fruit! In Africa, we were never allowed to bring it into the house as it brought bad luck! Imagine my joy when I moved to France to find it brought just the opposite there; *honeysuckle*: because if one were on a 'desert' island, one might just have to suck the honey from the flower for sustenance!

The red flower of the *aloe*: because, in the Transkei, the natives dye their blankets with the red of the flowers in order to be camouflaged among them and by them – hence the name, 'the red blanket country'; *rosemary*: because, not only is it for remembrance but it is indispensable in the kitchen, fabulous as a hedge and insurpassable to go to sleep with as its scent wafts through the windows to carry one off onto an overperfumed Cloud Nine!

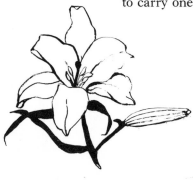

Joshua Logan

NEW YORK CITY
Theatrical director and producer

Wisteria; *cashmere bouquet*; yellow *jasmine*; *honeysuckle*; *night blooming cereus*; *magnolia* (grandiflora); *dogwood*; *clematis* (all forms); *anemone*; *stephanotis*.

Shirley Lord

NEW YORK CITY
Vogue editor

My island is abloom with flowers and of necessity, like Madeira, it has many different altitudes!

Violets (to remind me of Christmas in London); *mimosa* (ditto); *mistletoe* (ditto); *lily-of-the-valley*; white *roses*; *tuberoses*; *water lily*; *dogwood blossom*; *hibiscus*; *jasmine*. (If I didn't have my typewriter with me, I could at least create some perfume from this list!).

Clare Booth Luce

HAWAII
Author, playright,
US Ambassador to Italy, 1953–7

My favourite flower is, hands down, the incredibly glorious *night blooming cereus* (Hylocereus undatus (Haw.) Britt. and Rose – native of Mexico). The night blooming cereus does indeed bloom only after nightfall. Its petals are *pure white* and the leaves a dark green. When it opens *all the way* – which it does about midnight – the stamens stand quite free of the petals. It dies, alas, with the morning light.

Although I also love the traditional rose, the world's most popular flower, I know of no blossom that can compare in splendour to the night blooming cereus.

71

Stanley Marcus

DALLAS
Ex-President, Neiman-Marcus

Tulips; *tulips*; *tulips*; *tulips*; *tulips*; *tulips*; *tulips*; *tulips*; *tulips*; *anemones*.

Sir Henry Marking

LONDON
Chairman of the British Tourist Authority

Buddleia – because it attracts butterflies; *daffodils* – not so much for their brilliant colour and delicate scent, but mainly because of what they herald. They mark the end of the winter and the beginning of the new year in the garden. The first flowers I ever planted in land which belonged to me were daffodils and I felt it was all my own doing with no help from another when they finally showed their heads above the winter earth.

Geraniums – they are easy to grow; they are brilliant and they are lively; *honeysuckle* – I choose this because of its sweet smell, because it blooms over many months and because it stays green all the year round (at least, mine does) and – so far as I am concerned this is the most important consideration – it grows vigorously for even the most inefficient gardeners!

Hydrangeas – I have never had much success in growing hydrangeas but it may be that the soil on the 'desert' island would be more suitable than the soil in my garden. So I would certainly want hydrangeas, and I would hope that I could make them turn a brilliant blue. But even if they were pinky-red I should still like them; *lilacs* – I would want lilac bushes, both white and purple, because they combine exuberant growth with a delicious, strong smell; *lupins* – I would want some lupins because of the wonderful shadings and colour they have, more than any other flower.

Meadowsweet – is the sweetest smelling of all the hedgerow flowers. I always recall that near a tiny thatched cottage I used to own, meadowsweet grew in the hedgerows on each side of the lane, and its smell on a summer evening is not to be forgotten. I suppose even desert islands might have lanes and hedges too; *paeonies* – are extravagant flowers, extravagant in bloom and extravagant in leaf, and their faint, elusive and delicious scent all combine to mark the burgeoning of summer; *roses* – come alphabetically last on my list but they certainly rank first in my estimation because they combine the ultimate in form and colour and scent. But I certainly do not include under this heading those hateful flowers on long stems which florists sell and which masquerade under the name of roses but which have no smell and don't last long. I mean old-fashioned tea roses, and my favourite is Papa Meilland with its deep Burgundy velvet petals and almost overpowering scent!

Dame Alicia Markova

LONDON
Prima Ballerina

I have always had a passion for white flowers so I would have to take with me: *snowdrops*, white *tulips*, *lily-of-the-valley*, *Easter lilies*, white *daisies*, white *roses*, white *paeonies*, white *jasmine*, white *lilac* and *gardenias*.

Georges Mathieu

PARIS
Action painter

My tastes regarding flowers (as they do regarding women) vary every day.

When I was a little boy I was very fond of the *nasturtiums* which grew in the plat bands of my garden – maybe because they were so flat. However, I was intrigued by the *snap dragons*. Later, when I lived in Versailles, I had a passion for *glycines*. And I have memories of the gorgeous boxes full of *mimosas* that my mother used to receive from friends in Menton.

When I discovered the Riviera I was charmed by the sumptuous *bougainvilleas*. But today I have bought three bunches of *sweet peas* – purple, light purple and pink. On my balustrade, they illuminate the whole room. There is nothing like sweet peas (today)!

Dear Fleur,

My tastes regarding flowers (as they do regarding women) vary every day.

When I was a little boy I was very fond of the nasturtiums which grew in the plat bands of my garden – maybe because they were so flat.

However I was intrigued by the snap dragons –

Later when I lived in Versailles I had a passion for glycines.

And I have memories of the gorgeous boxes full of mimosas that my mother used to receive from friends in Menton.

When I discovered the Riviera I was charmed by the sumptuous bougainvilias

But to day I have bought three bunches of sweet peas purple, light purple and pink.

Placed on the balustrade of my triclinium they illuminate the whole room.

There is nothing like sweet peas!
(To-day)

My best wishes for your book
When are you coming to Paris?

Ma vie est triste sans Fleur.

affectueusement
vôtre
Georges

Clare Maxwell~Hudson

LONDON
Beauty expert

Jasmine; *honeysuckle*; *dog rose**; *poppy**; *anemone**; *passion flower**; *paeony**; *sunflower* – it not only looks wonderful but the seeds taste delicious; *daisy*; *tiger lily*.

* These are all useful medically – so they would not only look marvellous but also help keep one healthy.

Ian McCallum

BATH
Director of The American Museum in Britain

Rose: Lady Hillingdon, for climbing, Elizabeth of Glamis, for association; *fritillaria*: Snakeshead, for pattern and delicacy; *lily*: Enchantment, for elegance; *jasmine*: nudiflorum, for scent; *cymbidium*: Indian Tea, for a touch of the exotic; *camellia*: magniflora, for artifice; *columbine*: for nostalgia; *delphinium*: for show; *hellebore*: for something in the winter. P.S. With the last three, there are so many varieties that I am not specifying.

Mrs John A McCone

SANTA BARBARA, CALIFORNIA
Trustee, American Historical Society

My favourite flowers are: *Euphorbia wulfenii*; *matilija poppies*; *alstromeria*; *phlox*; *lily-of-the-valley*; white *violets*; *lilac*; *cymbidium orchids*; Sarabande-Floribunda *rose*; *wild flowers*.

Actually I love most flowers. For some reason I did not think you meant annuals so I did not include any on this list.

Henry McIlhenny

PHILADELPHIA, PENNSYLVANIA
Art collector and gardener

The flowers I like best are: *jade vine*; *nasturtium*; *lotus*; *lily-of-the-valley*; *amherstia nobilis*; tender-scented *rhododendrons* (brachystylum and crassum); blue *poppy*; *auratum lily*; *Magnolia grandiflora*.

Lady McIndoe

LONDON
Widow of Sir Archibald McIndoe

For beauty, pleasure and maybe survival: *poppy* – sleeping without pain; *foxglove* – heart; *witchhazel* – soothing; *angels' trumpets* – hallucination; *houseleek* – butterflies; *lime* – bees; *Strelitzia regina* – humming birds; *elderberry* – wine; *passion flower* – fruit; *primroses* – pleasure; *Naked Ladies*; *camellia*.

Zubin Mehta

NEW YORK CITY
Musical Director of the New York Philharmonic

Simply *jasmine*.

Sra Jorge Mellão

SÃO PAULO
Socialite

I love flowers so much that for a moment, in a vision, there I was in a dream island, surrounded by my favourites: *myosotis*; tea or red *roses*; *hibiscus*; *gardenias*; *bluettes*; *hortensias*; *mimosas*; *magnolias*; *peach flowers*; *rhododendrons*. Wished we could live among them, but only the beauty of friendship and love can be as rewarding as the flowers we praise.

Yehudi Menuhin

LONDON
Musician

Paeony; tea *rose*; *lily-of-the-valley*; *violet*; wild *narcissus*; *heliotrope*; *sunflower*; *apricot blossom*; *cornflower*; *Californian poppy*.

Hope Ridings Miller

WASHINGTON, DC
Author

Herewith is the list of flowers I'd choose to have on a lonely island, in order of preference:

Roses (like the one on your 1974 Christmas card); *violets*; pink *paeonies*; *pansies*; white *magnolias*; English *daisies* (of literary tradition); white *clematis*; wild *iris*; *foxgloves* (a source of digitalis, as you know); *bluebonnets* (perhaps because I'm a native Texan).

Mary Mitchell

JOHANNESBURG
Author

Do you know the creeper called pink *jasmine*? Well, I would hope to see it growing all over the island, festooning fallen tree trunks, climbing along any upright willing to support it; for not only has the creeper the daintiest little fern-like leaf and pale pink flowers, it is also prolific and the leaves never go 'off.' I have a sprig of the creeper before me as I write. How I wish I could capture the fragrance of the flowers and imprison it on paper! The flowers come out in our South African winter (June–July). They grow in clusters, each bloom tubular-shaped, with a head the size of a violet. When the flowers are open they are white; in bud they are an orchid-pink. Even when the flowers are open, their tubular stems, about an inch in length, are the same romantic pink. The scent . . . Our winters can be pretty bleak, though we are blessed with lots of sunshine; and when I see the first pink jasmine buds appear I feel quite nervous: will the fragrance have the same appeal as last year and all the previous years, or will it have staled and therefore lost some of its enchantment? I am never disappointed. For me, the perfume of pink jasmine is the epitome of hope, renewal.

Could there be several beds of *paeonies* on that mysterious island? Once I had to spend a long time in hospital. At that stage I'd never seen – I'd hardly heard about – paeonies! After the operation, when I started to surface, the bottom of my bed was a blur of white – a bowl of floppy, full-blown flowers. Ever since that day paeonies have reminded me that suffering, mental or physical, does not endure.

Nasturtiums, of course! I could eat the seeds and the leaves help to make delicious, nourishing salads. Not only do nasturtiums when in flower look like rivers of flame and molten gold, but they also have practical aspects. Think how future generations of islanders would benefit from their importation as food!

Not a bed, please, but whole fields of *carnations* or, rather, fields of green grass starred with the kind of carnations one hardly ever sees nowadays: gigantic creamy heads flecked with pink; monstrous crimson blossoms tipped here and there with white; flowers striped with gold and orange; all of them exuding the strong, spicy fragrance which of late seems to have vanished or been watered

down. Such proud, independent beauties would probably feel very much at home on the island where they could intermingle and perhaps – who knows? – grow even more exquisite and more fragrant with the passing years.

A myriad of hedges tangled with *dog roses*, creamy-gold, growing lushly. When it is hot and dry here in Johannesburg, when waking in the early morning I indulge in a favourite day-dream: in another climate (one that is soft and moist) I walk through a lane bordered with such hedges. The flowers (all of which have golden hearts) are cream and white. Dew lies upon their petals. Their scent is heady.

Violets, please, because they were the favourite of a lady I admire: the Empress Eugenie, wife of the third Napoleon. Born on the fifth anniversary of the death of the first Napoleon, her life spanned over ninety years. During the glittering, dissolute days of the Third Empire and, later, when she was an exile living in England, she knew much joy, much sorrow; and with the passing years I think she also became very wise. Certainly she was always gracious. There is a lovely story told about her. Because she put Charles Frederick Worth on the fashion map of Europe, so to speak, every year on her birthday, the 5th of May (even when she was in exile), the House of Worth presented her with a new dress plus a bunch of Parma violets. The House of Worth also created specially for her a perfume redolent with the scent of violets that is still sold today, 'Je Reviens.' Eugenie, it is true, never did return to France as Empress but, in later years, she often visited the country as a guest. After the first World War, not long before her death, she was honoured by the Government of France for her services to the sick and wounded. Having known many tributes of the empty kind this is an acknowledgement I feel the Empress would have treasured.

Camellias, every kind and colour – single, double, frilled edges, flecked, plain. Their natural habitat, I believe, is on the slopes of far-distant mountains. There, year by year, nourished by the thick, rich humus in which they stand, watered by rain nearly every day, they grow to incredible heights, while their blossoms are enormous. There is bound to be a mountain or two on the island. How magical it would be if the slopes were covered with camellia groves! I must also confess I love an opera, a play, a film and a book all associated with camellias. I've seen Greta Garbo's *Camille* at least six times, and listening to *La Traviata* is always transporting. No island could be absolutely lonely if one was surrounded by a tangible reminder of such joys.

On those boggy patches on the island, how *water irises* would grow and flourish! In September, our spring, they grace so many gardens with their long stems starred with pale blue ethereal-looking blossoms. They are just as enchanting when picked and brought indoors. Here again, given the right conditions, they ask for little. I think that perhaps they remind me of another life – but just where it was centred and what it involved, I cannot say.

There would have to be pink *magnolias* because, like camellias, their natural habitat is on mountain slopes and in far distant valleys: tall trees, literally laden with glorious pink blossom. The rose-pink magnolia, Sir Sacheverell Sitwell tells us in *Cupid and the Jacaranda* (a book that is a never-failing source of inspiration), once had such a special place in the world of art that if an old flower book had drawings in it of the magnolia species, it at once went up into another category of price. The flower is so beautiful, he feels, that it could have called a whole school of painters and poets into being – men and women who did nothing but paint and write about flowers and blossoming trees. Could there be a wiser choice than to associate oneself with such archetypal matter?

I pray there are lots of *hibiscus* bushes growing on the island; after all, does not one associate the hibiscus with exotic places? In Zimbabwe, where I spent my childhood, hibiscus were common flowers and it is only in the last decade or so that I have come to regard them with the reverence they merit. Then I perceived that although they are hardy and easy to cultivate, their blossoms do in fact have marvellous beauty, possessing a translucency and sheen few other blooms can equal. Also their variety nowadays is bewildering. So many hybrids have been perfected that there are hibiscus in nearly every shade of yellow, salmon, apricot, crimson, scarlet and vermilion. There are also white hibiscus, but these are rare. Their shape varies greatly too. Some are single, large, almost as big as soup plates; and there are double hibiscus that resemble bells; some are small and dainty – miniatures one could call them; some have edges that are slightly frilled, and some are plain. Now and then one finds blossoms that look as though silver or gold dust has been blown upon them. Something else: whether they are plucked, or whether they are left blooming on the tree, their life is short. One day, two days at the most, is their span. Whether the container that holds the picked hibiscus is dry or whether it is filled with water makes no difference to the period they grace our lives. Even in death they are graceful, for they do not shed their petals, like the rose for instance – instead they gradually furl themselves until they look for all the world like neatly rolled umbrellas.

Finally, the hibiscus is a flower that I have chosen to adopt as a personal symbol. It came, unbidden, in a dream, a gift from the gods; and, on reflection, in all the world I do not think one could ask for a better pledge, a more alluring symbol, for all that the life of the flower is so short as to be merely a passing thought.

S.A.S. Princess Caroline of Monaco

Paeonies, because they have no smell; blue Nile *rose*, because it's blue; *camellias*; *gardenias*; *azaleas*; *geraniums*; white *roses*; *lilac*; little pink *roses*; big pink *roses* – then I've roughly got my garden.

The Late
S.A.S. Princess Grace of Monaco

Here is my list in answer to your request for my ten favourite flowers: *zucchini flower*; *bamboo* (I hope you will accept it although I have never seen it flower); *rose*; *iris*; *lavender*; *rosemary*; *apple blossom*; *daisy*; *gladiolus*; *water lily*.

I chose zucchini so that I could eat the flower . . . let the leaves grow over a trellis made from the bamboo where I would sit quietly in the shade and contemplate my beautiful roses and pure white iris. Bees would make a hive in the fragrance of my apple tree and enjoy the lavender and rosemary to make their honey. After running through my field of daisies, I would stretch out . . . sip a little rosemary tea and nibble on a gladiolus bulb (very rich in Vitamin C). I would be very kind to this much maligned flower whose sisters are bobbing up and down, precariously perched on the back decks of yachts in Monte Carlo Harbour, looking quite forlorn. I would try to find a fresh water pond on the island for my water lilies with the hope that their large leaves will attract frogs. Who knows? One might turn into a handsome prince who would be decent enough to whisk me off this lonely island and take me back to civilisation . . . After all, I am really a city girl at heart!

Jean Muir

LONDON

Fashion designer

Bright red *geranium*; *garden pinks*; almost any *tulip*; almost any *lily* (especially white lilium candidium!); *lily-of-the-valley*; wild English *rose* and/or *old* garden roses (not modern hybrids); white 'common' *daisies* – growing; *primroses* – growing; *snowdrops* – growing; and, if allowed for luck, some moorish *heather*!

P.S. It would be lovely to possess: Dürer's 'Violets'!!; Nicholas Hilliard's 'Portrait of a Gentleman'!!; and a Stanley Spencer windowsill 'Geranium' . . . (three paintings). What a lovely game to play.

Lady Rupert Nevill

UCKFIELD, SUSSEX

Widow of Private Secretary to HRH Prince Philip

Here are the ten flowers that I should like to find in my survival kit for the 'desert' island; a small botanical nosebag. I think these would at least give me a sense of time and the passing year, and an insistent desire to return before too long to my native shores.

I would want to plant *snowdrop*, because it signals spring and is perfectly pure, with bells like breathing porcelain. The smell is so subtle. Then I would like to find *Daphne odora* with painted leaf and divinely scented waxen flowers, and follow this with the shyly-scented wild *violet*.

I would be unhappy without the *cowslip*, gracefully slender and smelling of meadow and earth. Nor could I manage for company without *violas* (or *pansies*), with faces of magical fantasy and all the pleasure inhaled when the summer rain drums out the scent from their leaves.

I would be very unhappy without the *rose*, but to single one rose above all others presents a problem. It is almost impossible to solve, even insensitive, but I think I could just manage to choose Roserie de l'Haye, a heady carmine velvet flower with delicate petals set in bright green, strongly indented leaves. It is powerfully scented and flowers over a very long season.

It would be an appalling diminishment not to plant the August *buddleia*. Its wonder lasts for at least three weeks, with silvery leaves and pale lilac horns. The scent would fill the island, invading every corner with honeyed sweetness. And a haze of fluttering butterflies would add yet another beautiful dimension to the bush.

With autumn turning towards winter, I would like to have the scented comfort of a storm-resistant *honeysuckle*. Perhaps it could twist and curl round my little bamboo house. Beside this house I would like to plant a sentry, the shiny-leaved *Magnolia grandiflora*. It would flower away into the new year, occasionally puffing its lemon scent through the palm fronds thatching my roof.

Finally, I would like to have Roman *hyacinths*, with their fragile white bells and light green leaves. I would love them to be planted in woven baskets, pushing through damp earth and moss and, mixed with the scent of wood fires and burning coconuts, they would fill me with a sense of winter comfort and gratitude for the continual rhythm of seasonal bounty.

I have tried very hard to keep my choice within your boundary of ten and have found it difficult to discard so many old favourites, but I have been guided by the sense of season and of sight, and the necessary feeling for coolness in a hot and possibly dry island (all 'desert' islands are hot and palm-fringed). The quality of flower has to be cool and tactile and sometimes exciting to the eye as well as to the skin.

Scent is so important. It would keep one's mind occupied with happy memories and in touch with home. They must be rewarding and flowers that you can have a relationship with, without a hint of cliché or tropical vulgarity. It wouldn't matter if they were quiet and didn't pop their seeds in the hot sun, nor swish or sigh in the wind, because the tropical vegetation would do all of that for one.

I have chosen them for their company, their hope and their nutritional value for mind and body because they would even taste delicious dipped in dew. So, for me, they have a certain kind of all-around feeding quality which one would need as a displaced person living on alien soil.

Nanette Newman

WENTWORTH, SURREY
Actress and author

I would like all the flowers on my island to grow in wild profusion – nothing neat and tidy. I would have a field of *poppies, daisies* and *cornflowers* growing in the distance amidst corn. Then other fields of *buttercups* (I always have baskets full in the house for the short time they are in season) because I think they are beautiful and underestimated.

Then I would choose *lily-of-the-valley* because I love their perfume and because they would bring back happy memories. Also lots of trailing and climbing pink *geraniums* (no red ones), full-blown white *paeonies* and beds of *forget-me-nots*. I would also want *snowdrops* if the island climate allowed! I don't like orchids but I do like *orchid trees* (or do I mean tulip trees?) such as one sees in Barbados.

I suppose I would have liked to have included roses, but seem to have reached my limit – but I think I would have to cheat and find some way of smuggling some *roses* on to my island.

Beverley Nichols

RICHMOND, SURREY
Author and garden authority

What a lovely idea! Here is my list. With the exception of the bougainvillaea, it is firmly British. The only thing that may make it unusual is that I do *not* put roses first. I think that the average garden is greatly 'over-rosed'. The whole idea, of course, is only a dream because one couldn't grow snowdrops and bougainvillaea together. Or perhaps *you* could! My list, in order of priority, is as follows: *lilium regale*; *bougainvillea* (common magenta variety); double purple *lilac* (Souvenir de Louis Spaeth); *camellia* (Donation); *rose* (Fragrant Cloud); *snowdrops* in clumps (Galanthus ebroessii); *agapanthus* hybrids; *English primroses* in clumps; *English bluebells*; *philadelphus* (Belle Etoile).

David Niven

VAUD, SWITZERLAND
Actor and author

Here's my little list: *daffodils*; *tulips*; *night-scented jasmine*; *hibiscus*; *lilacs*; *narcissi*; yellow *roses*; *lupins*; *delphiniums*; *marigolds*.

Lord Olivier

LONDON
Stage and screen actor and director

At the moment my gardening mind is filled with *roses*, so let me offer you a dozen of these:

Papa Meilland, Virgo, Panorama Holiday (an exquisite pink – common name is 'beautiful flower'), Prima Ballerina, Mischief, Super Star, Blue Moon, King's Ransom, Super Sun, Lady Belper, Queen Elizabeth Yellow, Queen Elizabeth Pink.

Thirteen – one more, bad luck or not – you are bound to feel it is lucky if it includes Julia's Rose.

Mme Vijaya Lakshmi Pandit

DEHRADUN, INDIA
Indian High Commissioner to the UK, 1955–61,
President UN, 1953–4, Ambassador to USSR, 1947–9,
to Ireland, 1955–61, to Spain, 1958–61

These are the flowers I can always live with, and the reasons why. First of all, *roses*. The rose, apart from its beauty, its variety and fragrance, has always been symbolic to me of the things I value most in life, and I love it above all other flowers. It is a reminder to me of my brother, Jawaharlal (Nehru), and all that he stood for, for he wore a red rosebud in his buttonhole every day, and it came to be associated with him as his special insignia. There are few days in the year when there is not at least one bowl of roses in my home.

Carnations thrive in India and I never tire of their colours and their spicy scent. I would be happy with them on a lonely island.

I am fond of *chrysanthemums* of all kinds, especially the big ones –
I think they are known as cambria – as, also, the tall, delicate, spiky
ones, and the small pompoms. Chrysanthemums are sophisticated
flowers, but the cambria and pompoms would not, I think be out
of place on an island, a great bank of them! Once during the late
autumn, which is the chrysanthemum season in India, I had a
particularly good showing of the cambria variety all along my
verandah and the steps leading to the garden. A friend who had had
one over the allowed number and was in a happy mood, mistook
them in the moonlight for policemen with their white turbans, and
came back to ask me why I wished to be guarded in this fashion!

Sweet peas are unassuming, fragrant and beautiful. I like to have
them around me, as also *paeonies* and *narcissi*. The narcissus figures
in Indian love poetry, and even a few of these modest-looking
flowers can overwhelm a room with their heady scent.

Tulips I love. They do not grow in our plains but they flourish in
the mountains and are especially lovely in Kashmir. On any
isolated island I would like a carpet of gay tulips, as well as *lilies*
of all kinds and colours, masses of them: white and yellow, pink
and red, plain and striped, sending forth their delicious perfume.
And no garden would be complete for me anywhere without a bed
of big *pansies*, purple and gold, with their speaking faces.

I think it is appropriate that I should end with the most utterly
serene of all flowers – the *lotus*. The Buddha has been likened to it,
'as calm and brilliant as the lotus that rises in the midst of the
waters'. That calm and brilliance would companion me, I know,
in the presence of lotuses on my island.

Norman Parkinson

TOBAGO
Photographer

My favourites: *petrea*; *datura*; *rose* – Eglantine wild rose of England
and the centifolias *only*; *wallflower* (blood colour); *hyacinth*; *passion
flower*; *Cheddar pinks*; *violet*; germander *speedwell*; *meconopsis
baileyi*.

Mrs Charles Percy

WASHINGTON, DC

Wife of the US Senator from Illinois

Fragrant flowers I adore: from *narcissus* in a front hallway as you open the door in winter, to *violets* on fur in the snow.

Tropical flowers are a must – the beautiful *frangipani*, of which leis are made; and the Sri Lankan Kandy Dancer *orchid* (although it doesn't have a fragrance); and, in Tunisia, the double *jasmine* which the vendors sell to you in beautifully arranged clusters, usually with one tucked behind their ears.

Bulgarian *roses* are a must and, to end, I'd love to be in the Shalimar Garden overlooking the lake at sunset in India, as it's truly one of the beauty spots of the world.

Countess of Perth

STOBHALL, SCOTLAND

I am sure you have noticed that gardeners always write to each other in green. Here is my list: *roses* (hybrid tea); *sweet peas*; *primulas*; *lily-of-the-valley*; *delphiniums*; *lilies*; *pinks*; *gentians*; *paeonies*; *trillium*.

Duarte Pinto Coelho

MADRID

Interior designer and Consul of Malawi

Sweet peas – for their scent and variety of colour; *orchids* – white cymbidiums, because they are so 'waxy and luxurious'; old-fashioned *roses* – particularly Queen Elizabeths for their fiery quality; *carnations* – just to remember how terrible the Portuguese Revolution was (carnation was the flower of the revolution); *sunflower* – so rustic, still so striking in a bouquet; *lilacs* – ordinary mauve, for their scent and their remembrances of the garden of my youth; *camellias* – because I love the tree and the foliage in contrast to the delicacy of the flowers; *zucchini flower* – so delicious to eat and yet so lovely to look at; *frangipani* – as it was the first flower to be used to make perfume (by the Egyptians); wild *iris* – because, in my youth, all the countryside around Cascais, where I was born, were covered with them in yellow and purple (now there are only houses).

Arpad Plesch

BEAULIEU-SUR-MER, FRANCE
Banker, patron of botanists

Datura – arborea; *erythrina* – Crista-galli; *hibiscus* – rosa-sinsenses; *camellia* – japonica; *strelitzia* – nicolai; *stephanotis* – floribunda; *digitalis* – peupera; *aristoclochia* – grandiflora; *gardenia* – jasmin-oides; *mimosa* – pudica; *nelumbium* – speciosum.

Roy Plomley

LONDON
Broadcaster of *Desert Island Discs*

Roses; *lily-of-the-valley*; *London Pride*; *violets*; *pansies*; *snowdrops*; *forget-me-nots*; *honeysuckle*; *nasturtiums*; *Michaelmas daisies*.

Mary Jane Pool

NEW YORK CITY
Editor

If I could only have one flower, I would want the island to be a field of fresh white daisies. Meanwhile, here are my ten favourites: white *daisies*; red *amaryllis*; purple and yellow *pansies*; big, full-blown white *roses*; pale pink *begonias* with pale green leaves; lavender *rothschildianas orchids*; tangerine *hibiscus*; purple and red *anemones*; *primulas*; *lily-of-the-valley*.

Sra Maria Portinari

RIO DE JANEIRO
Art critic

My favourite flower is the *camellia*. I do love its shape and it makes me think about the heroine of Alexandre Dumas fils' famous novel. The camellia is cool, aristocratic, *raffinée*, a symbol of what Marguerite Gautier would have liked to have been despite her modest origin and her way of life.

My second choice would be the red *rose*, a flower of passion which I relate to Spain, the country of my family. It also represents sensuous music, *corridas* and flamenco dance, as well as Carmen, the heroine of Merimée's novel and Bizet's opera.

The *orchid* comes in third place; it is a strange flower, full of mystery like a tropical goddess. The next would be the *daisy*. It is a naive flower, matching very well with children, and it is also the flower that I often buy for Denise, my daughter – she is very fond of *Giselle*, a famous romantic ballet in which the heroine tries to learn if she is really loved by a nobleman taking one by one the petals of a daisy.

Then comes *jasmine*. I adore its perfume, scenting all the house like a wild garden. The sixth is the *iris*, very poetic and graceful in shape. Then the *violet*, especially for its colour and delicate shape. The eighth is the *daffodil*, linked to the legend of Narcissus, a young man obsessed with his own beauty. For me, as an art critic, it also represents the loneliness of creation.

Then comes the *carnation* for a very simple reason: my grandmother always had a vase of carnations at her house where I spent pleasant days as a little girl. Number ten is the pink *gladiolus*. I received gladioli when I was a ballet student dancing for the first time on stage. It was also the flower decorating the church for my wedding.

Harold Prince

NEW YORK CITY
Theatre producer

Daisies; *roses*, of course (preferably yellow); *African violets*; those miniscule *Japanese orchids* – more bark than flower (I like those the best); *chrysanthemums*; *anemones* (second favourite); *lily-of-the-valley*; *cactus flowers*; *lilacs*; *tulips*.

Lady Pulbrook

LONDON
Florist

This is the most difficult task I've ever had! I love practically all flowers. Getting down to a short-list – carving out to make a list of ten – makes me feel a traitor!

I must have flowers that smell lovely and I'd want colour all the year round but, presuming my island would grow anything when I wanted it, I would pick the following – I think:

Anemone hupehenis: tall, graceful; *paeonies* – all colours, all types; *roses*: all colours (floribunda and old-fashioned); *lily-of-the-valley*: they smell so lovely; *Alchemilla mollis*: lovely, green beautiful to arrange with flowers (it also seeds itself with no trouble); *tulips*: double and single; Regale *lilies*: beautifully-formed trumpets with lovely smell; *sweet peas*: free-flowering and in such lovely colours; *Iceland poppies*: (must remember to burn the stems after cutting!); *narcissus*: every type.

I'd always be thinking of arranging them in vases and, for that, I'd love to include many, many more!

Mary Quant

LONDON
Designer, fashions and cosmetics

Daisy (of course); *camellia* (white, pale pink and red); *magnolia*; *iris* (purple); *azalea* (the sort that grow ten feet tall); *Madonna lily*; *poppy* (the simple wild one); *lavender*; *mimosa*; *geranium* (but only bright red).

Mrs Ronald Reagan

WASHINGTON, DC

I'd *love* to play the flower game with you! My favourite ten flowers
I'd like to take anywhere with me are:
    Lily-of-the-valley; *sweet pea*; *freesia*; *ranuncula*; *anemone*;
hyacinth; *lilacs*; *paeonies*; *roses*; *violets*. They're really my favourites!

Paige Rense

LOS ANGELES
Editor-in-Chief of
Architectural Digest and *Bon Appétit*

My schedule leaves me little time for strolling in the garden. My
garden, therefore, must come into the house. These are the ten
flowers I would – and do – invite to make themselves at home with
me.

In the entrance hall: *day lilies*, because their gold and yellow
and russet tones harmonise with my décor. But especially because
their botanical name, hemerocallis (meaning 'beautiful for a day')
reminds me of the magic of the present moment, of how much
one day can produce of beauty, creativity and glamour.

In the living-room: the *moth orchid*, for its exquisite form, its
air of serene sophistication and its classic marble whiteness.

In the study: the *fuchsia*, to which the Japanese give the name of
'lantern flower' because of its pendant blossom. Its diversity of
form and colour bestow a quiet richness upon a room that is, by its
very nature, a quiet place.

In the dining-room: floating in a shallow Lalique bowl, white
hibiscus blossoms. With just a whisper of pink at the throat, they
are delicate enough in colour, dramatic enough in form, for any
setting whether simple or elaborate. And of course there is no
fragrance. When food is served, that should provide the only aroma.

In the sitting-room: blending with the casual textures of canvas
upholstery and rush matting, fresh, cheerful *daisies* in a pottery
bowl and, in a slender vase, *daffodils* and *freesias*.

In the kitchen: nothing is more evocative of a summer morning
than the sharp and sprightly colours of *nasturtiums*. They look
good enough to eat – and of course they are – the stems and leaves
add a piquant flavour to salads; and the petals, used as a garnish,
are bits of shredded sunshine.

In the dressing-room: the sensual fragrance of *gardenias*, too long maligned as the 'prom corsage'.

In the bedroom: the *camellia* – sculptured repose – is to me the perfect flower for this room because it is delicate, feminine, romantic – and without aroma. I love the scent of flowers but not in the bedroom; here I want my own perfume to be the dominant fragrance.

The Duke of Richmond and Gordon

GOODWOOD, SUSSEX
Landowner and painter

Of course I'd love to play a game of flowers with you! It's very difficult to choose because all flowers are beautiful when they are not man- or woman-handled into some of those ghastly flower arrangements you find in hotels, artless houses or banqueting halls!

In this 'desert' garden I should hope to have a wall climbed by a gorgeous *Magnolia grandiflora*, as well as another *stellata* (the chap that flowers in April before its leaves) and at its other end I'd have copious *honeysuckle* with some banksia *roses* between.

Aside of this wall a great clump of *rhododendrons*, red and white, with their dark green leaves making a backdrop to some flowering shrubs like *senecio* and *Hypericum hidcote*. An *escallonia* or two somewhere here, especially the lovely 'apple blossom' one.

But I really believe well in the foreground I'd have *paeonies* in several large groups. And in front of these lots of low-growing ground cover – *St John's wort* and, oh yes, *periwinkles*. I believe periwinkles are almost the prettiest ground cover there is.

That gives you or, rather, me (!) about ten, and they're virtually flowering shrubs. Potting out is not for me and I'd be too lazy anyway on that 'desert' isle!

S. Dillon Ripley

WASHINGTON, DC
Secretary of the Smithsonian Institute

There are so many choices of attractive flowers that one could think of that it is very hard to suggest a group of ten. However, I have put together this brief list and my choices, while rather traditional, are things that I really love:

Tree *paeony*; any of the flowering species of *daphne*; any of the *pinks*; *delphinium*; *lilies*, especially the Near Eastern species; *iris*; *pansies* or *violas*; *clematis*; *roses* (especially the Near Eastern musk roses); *water lily* or *lotus*.

Lynda Johnson Robb

MCLEAN, VIRGINIA
Wife of the Governor of Virginia

It is very difficult to list my favourite flowers. I love the *geranium*; *rose*; *narcissus* (daffodil and jonquil); *tulip*; *daisy*; *anemone*; *begonia* and *zinnia* – but I also must add my favourite three flowering plants: the *magnolia*; the *dogwood* and the *azalea*.

Mrs Peter Rochelle Thomas

HAMILTON, BERMUDA
Collector

At first your invitation to play the flower game sounded like something very simple to do. However, I never realized how many flowers were my favourites. After writing down my initial list, I saw that this piece of geography would have to be the size of Australia and not a small 'desert island'. Playing 'flower games' is a temptation I could not refuse and I submit my abbreviated list herewith.

Gerbera daisy – my most favourite flowers, especially in the palest shades of pink, salmon, white and yellow; *Hindu lotus* (nelumbo nucifer) – words like tranquillity and serenity seem so appropriate to describe these lovely flowers. Even the leaves have a most appealing shape; Gloriosa *lily* – these are fun to watch as they open. I get the impression that Dali would reconstruct a parrot tulip to look like this; Sunburst *sunflower* – I love the tousled appearance of this flower. It will also serve a purpose by producing seeds which, one hopes, will attract all sorts of birds; Royal *poinciana* – I cannot imagine living anywhere without a tree, especially one that looks like a floral umbrella. The leaves are so delicate in cool shades of green.

Freesia – it would be nice to have a carpet of these fragrant flowers under the poinciana; *Dombeya* (hydrangea tree) – another tree, please. This one is very amusing because it has drooping pink balls of flowers that look like Christmas ornaments. It is best viewed standing beneath it. Oh yes, it very appropriately does bloom at Christmastime; *Nasturtium* – a cascade of these flowers are a beautiful sight. I love the saucer-shaped leaves; *Hibiscus* (Southern Belle) – I have grown this flower and certainly it must be seen to be believed. The flower is immense, ten and a half inches in diameter but, unfortunately, it only blooms for one day (just long enough for one to run out of film!).

Geranium – 'Old Faithful', it seems, for, when all other flowers fail for some reason or another, these survive. Those with scented leaves of lemon, apple, rose and coconut are fun.

H & Mrs Archibald Roosevelt Jr

WASHINGTON, DC
Chief of protocol at the White House

Freesias; *anemones*; *jasmine*; *lily-of-the-valley*; *daffodils*; *hyacinths*; *lilacs*; *wisteria*; *tulips*; *roses* (anything, but red).

Lanning Roper

LONDON

Landscape designer and garden columnist

I find it terribly difficult to list my ten favourite flowers as I think of them in so many different ways – garden plants, house flowers, scent, etc.

Alchemilla mollis; *marguerites*; *rosa rugosa* Blanc Double de Coubert; *Lilium auratum platyphyllum*; *Iris pallida dalmatica*; *Narcissus poeticus* (pheasant's eye); *Lavender*; white *paeonies*; *Magnolia denudata*; *Prunus subhirtella autumnalis*.

Mary, Viscountess Rothermere

MONTE CARLO

Socialite

How impossible to choose only ten flowers for that 'desert' island! And how like you to present such a challenge and so much fun. I've been thinking about it ever since except before lunch; then the flowers that delight are quite different and only concern cuisine!

My island would be Cipango where Marco Polo searched for the Fountain of Youth. It would be nearly hidden by masses of *columbines* of all colours and sizes. Beyond would be a field of *lavender*: Munstead blue with paths to walk through and to listen to the bumblebees buzzing. I could dry the blossoms to scent my bath water.

Even on Cipango one would need privacy (hoping not to be alone!). I should plant *Choisia ternata*, not only because the flowers have such a pretty scent but also because the leaves are a fresh green and it grows into thick hedges very quickly. Bordering the hedge there would be *fuchsias*, because I love them. I like Capri the best because it blooms in the autumn and the buds look like Chinese lanterns.

Don't you think you'd like to sense the change of the seasons? For Spring I'd choose *apple blossom*, perhaps the one discovered at Blenheim. There'd be fruit to eat later on for me and the birds – and cider. And that wood smells so delicious when it burns. Away in the distance there'd be Spanish *chestnut blossom*. Impossible to live on apples alone! With *lily-of-the-valley* scattered, like stars, in the wood below. And I think I'd grow *coriander* beside the woods. Herbs are always useful and these miniature blossoms and lovely-tasting leaves are fantastic. They get peppery when they are dried. No plant I know has a more exciting history – it was the first word Sir Arthur Evans recognized on the Rosetta Stone and it enabled him to translate Linear B.

Even further away, the Mexican '*Maguey*', agave americana. Perhaps I have too many white flowers; I do, but they are so tranquil and always more scented than others. The blossoms weren't as important in Mexico as the leaves in the old days because the tip is like a tiny quill which one can use to write on the fleshy base. I'd have to make a calendar and a map of the stars, and write the poems and prayers one remembers. Also from the roots there is a sort of liqueur, medicinal of course.

Being Southern, I'd like to plant some Confederate *jasmine*, or *Trachelospermum jasminoides*, to wander over the rocks. I have always had it since I grew up and started my own garden. There's some growing here on the balcony in Monte Carlo.

I wanted to save the best for last. I could not choose my most favourite *rose* but I know that if I could only have one it would be Danse de Feu. It is a carmine colour, and scented too. Do you remember the *Rubaiyat*:

> Look to the rose that blows about us – 'Lo
> Laughing,' she says, 'into the world I blow:
> At once the silken tassel of my purse
> Tear and its treasure on the garden throw.'

Mala Rubinstein

NEW YORK CITY
Cosmetician

I love almost all flowers – with very few exceptions. My *first* choice:
anemones – in great abundance – for the richness of colours (almost
all French painters did it); *mimosa* – the fragrance and beauty
always reminds me of the Côte d'Azur; *lilac* – a tree next to our
house in Cracow, Poland (I also love lilacs mixed with tulips in a
variety of colour). *Rose* – my sentimental attachment to one flower
in a vase, inspired by André Maurois' book *Climat* (the heroine
used only a white rose but I enjoy any colour, and am thrilled with
the rose named after me in Regent's Park, London); *lily-of-the-
valley* – how lavishly you used them on your Sussex country table
for lunch – they are so delicate; *orange blossom*; a *fig tree* (for the
foliage and for eating!); a *grape fruit tree* (ditto); a *lemon tree* – I
love the leaves!; and *chestnut trees* – to form a long guard to my
entrance.

Oh well, my dream world!

Mrs John Barry Ryan

NEW YORK CITY
Socialite

I love all the spring flowers best: *narcissus*; *tulip*; *daffodil*; *pansy*;
hyacinth; *forget-me-not*; *stock*; *lilac*; *iris*; *canna lily*.

The Rt Hon
Norman St John Stevas MP

LONDON
MP and former Minister

Lilies; *lily-of-the-valley*; *freesias*; *violets*; *daffodils*; *primroses*;
azaleas; *camellias*; *jasmine*; *bougainvillea*.

Marie-Louise Scio

ROME

Latin American editor of US *Harper's Bazaar*

How would I get to a 'desert' island and what flowers would I take? How would I feel alone? Questions of all sorts arose in my mind and stymied my imagination.

Would there be a graceful seashell drawn by four handsome seahorse to pick me up? Would I be in a white chiffon Grecian style gown or would I be in my pale oyster silk Fortuny dress with miles of hidden pleats, ready to catch and hold the wind for the sail across?

Surely the seahorses would be swift, gliding smoothly over foam-capped waves. The gentle spray would mingle with the fragrances of my flowers. I would surround myself with my bouquets and they would collectively cushion my sadness at bidding goodbye to my husband and children.

I see the island now. It is surprisingly small. The waters that surround it are turquoise, and the island itself an emerald green. The most precious of jewels could never capture the hues.

I am the first to arrive, or so it seems, so I can stake out the point where I can see the sun rising and the sun setting. The sand is silky but, miraculously, holds my first flower – *tuberose*. How majestic it looks there.

It seems to me to nod accordingly with my choice of *sweet jasmine*, and my fragrant *orange blossoms*. Where can I float my white *lily* pads? Ah, there they are in the sea of turquoise water. How right it all seems! The flowers seem to carry on some secret dialogue between themselves with cordial welcomes bestowed on each by the graceful bending of their stems.

My *gardenia* seems bruised. Did I wait too long to plant her? The *lily-of-the-valley* seems pleased with her selection; the white *lilac* bush seems bewildered at the new environment but, after some gentle – and soothing – comments from the tuberose, all is well.

There is a defiance in the air. Yes, the English *tea rose* is as white as she is cross. She'll soon learn to love the warmth and the sea! Ah, now she is transformed, opening gracefully as if to bow and apologize. The white *tulip* takes heart from the rose and immediately bends deeply in gratitude.

The white *carnation* is like pepper. Hot, spicy and definitely the cheery member of the group. She loves travelling and her perfume, momentarily at least, dominates the air.

In a moment, the sea will gather moonlight and each flower will hold summer in her winter's sleep.

Anne Scott-James

LONDON
Gardening authority

It is very difficult to pick ten flowers out of all the ones one loves. I have tended to pick the hardy flowers which have served me best over the years – my tenth is the only tender one in the list. I have put them roughly in their flowering order in England, though I don't know how they would behave in your 'desert' island!

Helleborus atrorubens (alternative choice *Eranthis hyemalis* – winter aconite); *Primula vulgaris* (primrose); *Narcissus cyclamineus* March Sunshine (alternative choice *Clematis macropetala*); *Fritillaria imperialis* (Crown Imperial); *Primula veris* (cowslip); *Alchemilla mollis*; *rose*, of which two of my favourites are climbing rose Mme Alfred Carrière' and shrub rose Mme Lauriol de Barny; *philadelphus* Belle Etoile; *cyclamen* Neapolitanum Album; *Jasminium polyanthum*.

Eric Sevareid

WASHINGTON, DC
Television political analyst

I have got into spring flowers for some reason – I guess to pretty up my rather stodgy suburban spot. So I plant *crocuses*, *daffodils*, *hyacinths*, *tulips* and *forsythia*. My wife has started a *gladioli* bed. I love *roses* of any hue, anytime; and I love the wild flowers that fancy up the dreary roadside stretches in Virginia, like the *daisies* and *Black-eyed Susans*, and the *cornflowers*. I don't like tropical-type flowers such as orchids; they are too fleshy and, when I cut one of them, I expect blood. I like northern hemisphere flowers, their freshness and the innocence of some.

Eugenia Sheppard

NEW YORK CITY
Society columnist, *New York Post*

I especially love *daisies*, because they are such happy, sturdy flowers and I associate them with my birthday which is always on a hot July day; I love *anemones* for their marvellous colours; I love violets, *lily-of-the-valley*, *nasturtiums* and *impatiens* which grows so profusely almost anywhere; I adore *jasmine* and *day lilies*, both the tiger types that grow along the roadside and the new pale beigey pinks that the florists have; I'm also very fond of *iris* in all shades; and *paeonies*. All flowers are wonderful but those that I have named appeal to me more than those that are more spectacular and exotic.

Beverley Sills

NEW YORK CITY
Director of the New York City Opera

Without my *gardenia*
My disposition's far meanier.
So sweet is the *violet*
I could turn to a diabet.
I always better feel-ya
If I have a *camille-ya*.
Though I know the word's chancy
I'm wild for a *pansy*.
I'd want a *geranium*
But not on my cranium.
To keep me from going crazy
I'd need to have my *daisy*.
And to please my nose
A yellow yellow *rose*.
Would I be so silly
To omit a tiger *lily*?
Who would pardon my lack
If I left out the *lilac*.

But the one flower of all I really would miss is my darling Fleur, to whom I send a fat kiss.

Mary Sinclair

LOS ANGELES
Actress and painter

Freesias; *roses*; *paeonies*; *anemones*; *camellias*; *hyacinths*; *orchids*; *lilacs*; *wisteria*; *tulips*.

Roberto Sodre

SÃO PAULO
Recent Governor of São Paulo

My ten best loved flowers: first of all, *Fleur Cowles*; then *rose*; *chrysanthemum*; *victoria-regia*; *lilac*; *orchid*; *forget-me-not*; *violet*; *carnation*; *primrose* and *azalea*.

When will it be possible to visit this so special garden in the most special garden you have imagined?

Mrs Gordon Southam

VANCOUVER
Friend of the author

The first thing I would insist on planting on my 'desert' island is *grass*. Yes, of course it's a flower. You would soon find this out if your gardener left and you saw all those little white things instead of smooth rolling green turf. I need grass to walk on in my bare feet after the hot sand. Also, I must lie down on the grass and gaze up at my *cherry tree*, which will be covered with masses of pale pink fluffy blooms. What a sight to see the blue, blue sky through a sea of pink flowers. When the cherries come, I will have birds to eat them and I will feel right at home.

Around the base of the cherry tree, I shall plant masses of *impatiens* reds, pinks, whites, oranges and mauves. They look so wonderful together I feel they should be called 'cheerfulness', not impatiens. Just before the impatiens are at their best, I shall have *daffodils* coming up through the neat green grass. That is how daffodils should be seen! naturalized, in clumps, at their own whim, and not in prim borders. I'm also looking forward to my *roses*. Any roses. Tea roses, tree roses, moss roses, musk roses, wild roses, climbing roses, red, red roses! All are welcome to transform my desert island and keep me occupied tending them. That's half their joy.

After the pinks and reds and golds I must have *delphinium* in blues and purples to remind me of my father's grey granite wall, where they grew so strongly to six or seven feet tall. (I still have some of these very plants in our real-world garden on the west coast of British Columbia.) I shall plant lots of *paeonies* in pale pink, white and deep red. They are so sturdy and strong, with a heavenly perfume; also, they won't need much care (I don't want to be working *all* the time). Paeonies remind me of the time in my childhood when I picked all the fat round buds, took them to my mother in a basket and asked her if she'd like to play marbles with me! Although I hated being given that evening's meal in my room, I still love paeonies!

For something more casual and wild I'd have *poppies*: scarlet poppies for the brave Canadians buried in Flanders fields, orange poppies for my beloved California, blue and pink ones for my summer garden at Qualicum Beach. I'd plant *lilies*, spikes of stately ones – for their disciplined beauty and their faithful reappearance year after year. No trouble and a symbol of eternity to me.

I've saved my favourite for the last. *Freesias* mean love. They remind me of our naval wedding forty-one years ago, when both the church and our house were filled with white freesias. Every February since then, I only have to close my eyes, smell freesia and I am transported.

Mary Spain

LONDON
Poet

Having made a list of every flower I could think of, I then marked my favourites (eighteen of them) and finally, after much heart-searching, reduced the list to ten. I love informality in natural beauty and the idea of formal flower-beds on that island just didn't seem right. So the flowers I've chosen are not only my favourites but they are also ones that one could stumble across whilst exploring the terrain. It's impossible to give an order of preference, so here they are as they came to mind:

Water lilies – and a woodland pool, please; *freesias*; *narcissi*; *lily-of-the-valley*; *dog roses* – and a spreading hawthorn for them to riot over; *camellias*; *harebells*; wild *cyclamen*; *ipomoea*; *gentians* – and some rocky upland to find them on, please; (also-ran: wild marguerite!).

Terence Stamp

LONDON
Stage and film actor

My first conscious affair with a flower was with a pledge of the sun itself. Having succeeded in growing one taller than myself in our backyard, I was thereafter rarely without a pocketful of seeds which I sprinkled everywhere I went, dreaming of a day when I would be old enough to have my own passport and confess my occupation as Grower of *sunflowers*.

I must have been much preoccupied with height in those days, for my next crush was on the stately *hollyhock*. Pilfering seeds and the occasional irresistible growing specimen – almost black with double petals – to plant in my grandma's garden. Into her superior soil followed *lupins* and *snapdragons*.

A trip to Tattenham Corner, a whole day amidst an envelope of perfume with a sky of *bluebells* around my feet and a field of fragile *beech* leaves over my head, opened previously unknown vistas of appreciation.

Returning every year from the hop gardens of Kent with only Guy Fawkes to brighten the long academic horizon, it was always cheering to see clusters of *Michaelmas daisies*, the blue ones – Marie Blanchard I think – peering irreverently from behind our coping.

Wallflowers, especially those which grow out of walls and always seem to be the most fragrantly scented. That old fashioned purple-maroon *iris* that moves like an orchid but smells like plum-wine.

I have always wanted to inherit an ancient bower of *wisteria* into which I could grow a New Dawn *rose* and sit under it at tea-time.

How many is that, nine or ten? Well, masses of *sweet peas* to cool me down when I am overheating.

Mrs Marshall Steves

SAN ANTONIO, TEXAS
Amateur botanist

Freesia; *anemones*; *hibiscus*; *geraniums*; *Peruvian* and *butterfly lilies*; *gaillardia*; white *daisies*; *zinnias* (Sombrero – pinks, oranges, Old Mexico); Gloriosa *daisies*. For fragrance: *night-blooming jasmine*; Cape jasmine; Confederate jasmine; Maid of Orleans jasmine; *tuberose*; *honeysuckle*.

Thank you for causing me to discover that I like my very own place to bloom better than anywhere else on earth.

Mrs James Stewart

BEVERLY HILLS
Wife of the actor and film star

I find it almost impossible to leave any flower off my list. I love them all. However, here are our choices: Jimmy nods 'yes' when I mention the name of *any* flower. These are not in any particular order:

Iceland poppies; *paeonies*; *ranunculus*; *rhododendrons*; *lily-of-the-valley*; *tuberose*; *begonias*; *anemones*; *impatiens*; *camellias*.

Dorothy Stickney

NEW YORK CITY
Actress and writer

My favourite flower is *phlox*. I love it in all its different colours. My garden has purple and white and a brilliant pink.

Sir Roy Strong

LONDON
Director of the Victoria and Albert Museum

What a difficult question to ask as I look out on to my icy snow-bound acres! One is either a designer or a planter when it comes to a garden, and I'm the former and think more in terms of architecture, statuary, seats, colour, light and shade. When it comes to flowers, it's the grey garden, the white garden, the iris garden and so on, and scarlet and yellow are very dangerous colours of which a little goes a long way in a garden or on a canvas! My list is as follows. There are too many roses but I love them and cannot have enough cascading everywhere:

Parrot tulip (preferably green into white); *Lonicera* (any form of honeysuckle); Louise Odier (Bourbon *rose*); white *hyacinth* (any variety); *Dianthus allwoodii* Doris (or any form of old-fashioned garden *pink*); Albertine (rambler *rose*); Frühlingsgold (modern shrub *rose*); Iceberg (Floribunda or climbing *rose*); *violets*; *Lent lilies*.

The list is inevitably arbitrary and entirely personal, and is largely formed of what one actually grows. Perhaps they'd look a bit odd all together on that 'desert' island, but they'd make a change from listening to my eight records.*

Mrs John P Sundberg

WASHINGTON, DC
Educator

Fleur Cowles *rose*; *crab apple* (Malus floribunda); *weeping cherry*; *freesia*; *Pieris japonica*; *flowering plum*; *hawthorn*; *stephanotis*; *stock*; *rhododendron*.

---

* Referring to *Desert Island Discs* – Roy Plomley's popular BBC radio programme, on which invited guests name the eight records they'd take to a desert island – F.C.

Graham Sutherland

LONDON
The late painter

I choose the *primrose*, but I doubt very much whether they would grow on a lonely island except in a damp climate.

Helen Suzman

JOHANNESBURG
Opposition politician

For what it is worth here are the flowers I would choose to take to an imaginary 'desert' island:

African violets – to remind me of home; *poppies* – because they are so colourful and easy to pick; *daffodils* – for their smooth stems and beautiful blooms; *narcissus* – for scent wafted on the breeze; *bougainvillea* – to run riot; *artichokes* – because you can eat them; *sweet peas* – for obvious reasons; *iris* – bearded and otherwise; *hydrangeas* – there must be shade on the island; *dahlias* – because you can divide them.

Janet Suzman

LONDON
Actress

Here's what I'd like to take to this island: *sweet peas*; *freesias*; *roses*; *daisies*; *azaleas*; *lilac*; *poppies*; *flowering cherry*; *magnolias*; *poinsettias*.

Rufino Tamayo

MEXICO CITY
Distinguished painter

This is my list of flowers, but instead of ten I chose eleven, being plain *Fleur* the best of them all. The rest are as follows:
Amaryllis; *hibiscus*; any *cactus flower*; *canna lily*; *tiger lily*; *dahlia*; *yucca*; *lotus*.

Mrs P E Thompson-Hancock

LONDON
Fashion doyenne

Some *roses* – mostly Floribunda (pity the Rose Society has scrapped that lovely name): Iceberg, Jan Spak, Aileen Wheatcroft, Penelope, Fritz Noblis, New Dawn, and many others, especially old roses. Sacheverell Sitwell wrote: 'Rose prolifera, a centifolia or cabbage . . . the most beautiful of roses, sometimes too beautiful to be described. The drops of moisture, which in themselves are scented Rosewater . . . as we draw in our breath the sensation is animal – as of a lovely skin . . .'
Prunus – Plena, Iceberg, Tai-Haku, Shimidsu sakura, Yedo sakura; *camellia* – Alba simplex, J. C. Williams, Cornish Show; *pelargonium* – Doris Frith, Renoir, Carpelle, and many others; *magnolia* – all, I think, are lovely; *plumbago*; *clematis*; *jasmine*; *nasturtium*; *paeony*.

I would have liked to include ordinary garden white lilac and syringa – but think I have too many bushes!! And, really, no room for my wild flowers (those marked * in natural habitat only – the rest in the house, the garden): sea lily – marvellous scent, just grows in sand; *asphodel; Queen Anne's lace; eucalyptus; *cyclamen; *cistus; honeysuckle; *mimosa; cladanthus; iris.

Lady Thorneycroft

LONDON

Wife of the former Chairman
of the Conservative Party

Amaryllis; *hibiscus*; *rose*; white *water lily* (Nymphaea alba); *violet* (viola odorata, white and mauve); *jasmine* (white); *Magnolia stellata*: *lily-of-the-valley*; *lilac* (white and purple); *hyacinth* (white).

Mrs David Tiller

DALLAS

Publicist

So much has been said in poetry, prose, paintings and music about flowers through the ages that little language is left for present-day description. Therefore my thoughts are purely personal (and I've rearranged the list a thousand times since your note arrived).

Marguerite daisy: this heads my list for its innocent and universal beauty. It always seems right and, like the 'little black dress', it can always be dressed up or down. Since using the daisy in a special way (with maidenhair fern and jungle animals) planted the seeds for your and my garden of friendship all those years ago, I shall be eternally grateful to this cheerful flower.

Gaillardia pulchelia (firewheel or Indian paintbrush): I would have to take at least one Texas wildflower. As you know, one of the great ladies of our time, Lady Bird Johnson, introduced me to the quiet charm of the roadside flowers of Texas. The gaillardia is a favourite we shared among them. The days spent working, touring, entertaining and being entertained amid the grand fields and along the roadsides of the LBJ Ranch are forever in view through the windows of my mind.

Geranium: I always like to use the unexpected as a cut flower, and I place the geranium at the top of the list, especially as I know that it was one of the flowers the Empress Josephine brought to the gardens at Malmaison; *cornflower* (centaurea cyanus): For its electrifying blue. It's easy to see why it was a favourite Fabergé jewelled flower; *lily*: I like the imperial lily for its 'majesty'. Nothing to me is more graceful or rich with colour, and there would be four to choose from – auratum (for its splash of yellow), rubrum (brushed in peach), Enchantment (vibrant orange) and Peach Blush (for its delicate peach glow).

Paeony: said to be one of the oldest cultivated flowers in the world, it fits its Chinese name which means 'the most beautiful'; King Alfred *jonquil* or *daffodil*: Wordsworth said it more eloquently than I ever could:

'. . . For oft when on my couch I lie,
In vacant or in pensive mood,
They flash upon that inward eye
Which is the bliss of solitude;
And then my heart with pleasure fills,
And dances with the daffodils.'

Tulip: my Dutch ancestry cries out through my love of the tulip – especially the parrot tulip – in all its splendour. Alas, the blooms are not lasting, either potted or as a cut flower but we used them as a frequent party flower during my days at the LBJ Ranch; *ranunculus*: For their kaleidoscopic colours which enhance any bouquet.

Spring crocus: not so much for the way it looks but because it signifies the coming of spring and spirits are lifted in anticipation. I would always be reminded of my son's favourite bedtime story when he was very small – *The First Robin* by Robert Kraus. Tiny fingers have tattered and soiled this miniature book from *The Bunny's Nutshell Library*. The young bird in this story wants to be the first robin to see spring. So does our little fellow. No matter what lies ahead, I shall eternally link his young life with the crocus and Spring's first robin.

If one could choose what other things to take before being cast on the desert island, I'd like three containers to use interchangeably with such an assorted collection of flowers: A Lowestoft soup tureen in the tobacco-leaf pattern, an antique American pewter pitcher and an ash splint basket, characteristic of the late nineteenth century, a period I enjoy.

Phillip Tobias

JOHANNESBURG

Anthropologist and palaeontologist

Whatever will you get up to next? I am enchanted by the idea of joining you in a flower game. In my case, conditioned by my life in the sub-tropics and by what I have seen and learned to love in sub-Saharan Africa – from Nairobi to Durban – I have chosen flowers which are almost entirely tropical and sub-tropical. But then, if it is a remote and lonely island to which you are consigning me, it is more than likely that such island will be in the tropics or sub-tropics. That is entirely appropriate. I have assumed that the island is a volcanic one – namely, that it rises straight out of the sea, has a marine seashore rich with botanical life, and then soars up to a volcanic peak: so that I can put some high mountain species well above sea-level!

Anthericum; *bougainvillea*; *frangipani*; giant mountain *protea* (Protea grandiflora); giant *mountain lobelia*; *Golden Shower*; *poinsettia*; *Pride of India*; *red hot poker* (the flame flower); wild *orchids*.

Mrs Toni Tomita

MADRID

Friend of the author

Marguerites; *anemones*; *roses*; *tuberoses*; *lily-of-the-valley*; *jasmine*; *magnolia*; *lotus*; green *zinnias*; *jonquils*.

Pauline Trigère

NEW YORK CITY

Fashion designer

From the simple *trillium* to the modest *violet* or whatever flower grows, I love them all and could not enjoy life without them.

If I were to go to your imaginary desert island, I would never leave the *tulip* behind – the tulip which does my heart so good. To enjoy seeing it closed like a beautiful flute of champagne or, to admire it when proudly opened like a fabulous star.

Anemones would never be out of my imaginary garden – their rainbow colours mixing beautifully anywhere. Nor would delicate *freesias* with their enchanting scent.

Since your island promises to grow anything, what a delight it would be to be surrounded always with *day lilies* changing their hue constantly – the aphrodisiac odour of lilies and *liliums* would add a romantic aura to one's dreams at night.

And then the *roses*: how could I forget them – all of them, with their wonderful fragrance?

And the *Black-eyed Susans* . . . and the *astilbe* swaying gracefully on their long stems.

For me, any place without flowers is not any place at all.

Sra Piru Urquijo

MADRID
Socialite

Here is the list of flowers I would like to take to the lonely island where everything grows . . . the only snag about the island must be the distance it has to be from Spain, where *nothing* ever grows!! Here go my plants:

Mimosa; *jasmine*; *rose*; *lilac*; *daffodil*; *lily-of-the-valley*; *rosemary*; *thyme*; *rock-rose*; *heather*; *iris* (needless to say, I would need a gardener on the island too) . . .

Gérald Van der Kemp

PARIS
Director, restorations of the Palace of Versailles
and the home and gardens of Monet

Je m'empresse de rejoindre à votre gentille question! *Rose, iris, pivoine, pavot, lys, azalée, glycine, narcisse, crocus, cyclamen, tulipe.*

John Van Eyssen

NEW YORK CITY
Film producer

Primroses; *daffodils*; white *daisies*; *freesias* (indigenous to South Africa); English garden *roses*; a field of red *poppies*; purple *iris*; *lilac*; *anemones*; a white *cactus flower*.

Baroness Van Till

THE HAGUE
Authority on legal death

If I had to live on a lonely island for a long time, I'd want flowers the year round, so I'd choose:

Jasminum nudiflorum (yellow winter jasmine), for its courage to flower in winter, giving me the illusion that spring is around the corner; *snowdrops*, for the same reason; *mimosa*, for their light-heartedness; *camellias*, they flower after mimosa and anywhere, and are green in winter; two plague-resistant, strongly-perfumed *roses*, for their sensuousness and warmth: for instance, Wendy Cusson (red) and Chinatown (yellow); a white *hortensia* to light up an otherwise dark or sunless corner; a *Hydrangea petiolaris* (I mean the climbing kind) to decorate the north side of my hut; a few dozen (if permitted) parrot *tulips*, to remind me of the endless variation of life; some *primulas*, because they flower twice a year even in semi-shadow; a *flower of fantasy*, to be designed by Fleur Cowles: jubilant and discreet, light and strong, perfumed and soft to touch.

Robert Vavra

SEVILLE
Author of *Tiger Flower* and other
books written around Fleur Cowles' paintings

A red *Spanish poppy*, because they are much a part of me and have been so important to my photographs of horses; a *sunflower*, because they're so bright – and because their seeds are good to eat. Whenever anyone says 'sunflower,' even after this long time in

Spain and though they've appeared in many of my photographs, I think of your paintings of them: one in particular that is still clear in my mind; *jasmine*, because of its fragrance, because of its look and because the poetry of Garcia Lorca is important to me and I can't not associate it with jasmine.

A *magnolia tree*, because I associate it with Freemont Park in Glendale, California – two blocks from my home, and where I spent some of the happiest hours of my youth, sipping Hires orange and playing Monopoly on the grass under the trees. Also, the shade from the tree might come in handy on the island; the *California poppy*, because it's a lovely flower and because I also associate it with my youth. How tightly they close themselves up at night. When you look at a California poppy in the sunshine, Buffon's words ring so true: 'Nature is more beautiful than art . . .'

A *hollyhock*, because I associate it with those wonderful summers – not wonderful to me at the time – that I spent with my Grandmother Hamilton in the hick oil town of Taft, California which is right on the edge of Steinbeck country. How those hollyhocks, magenta in colour, ever grew in that pale, dry (it was hard too) soil of my Grandmother's front yard, I'll never know! But that flower would remind me of her and of an important part of my past; *geranium*, because my dad was an amateur gardener and we had lots of geraniums in our back yard – he was always giving people slips. Those were my first lessons in giving and if I were on an island and were visited by someone from another island, I'd like to give them a slip to take home with them.

A *jacaranda tree* – I've always been crazy about the colour of that tree's flowers and have no reason but that to take one to my island; white *Spanish daisies*, because without them the red poppies might appear pretty dull in a solid field of red.

The flowers from the cover of *Tiger Flower* – that is, the painting – which would, like the hollyhocks in my grandmother's garden, be a reminder of a person who has been very special in my life and who has had a hand in making my life special.

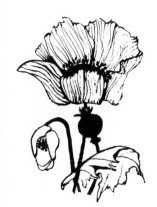

FLEUR '82

Victoria Wakefield

HAMPSHIRE
Gardener

Snowdrops (Elwisii in particular); *stephanotis*; *primroses*; *lilies* (if I have to choose one – Regale); *Erigeron mucronatum*; *Morning Glory* – must be Ipomoea Heavenly Blue (none of the others!); mixed *pansies*; *cyclamen* – persicum; *honeysuckle* – Lonicera tragophylla best; *rose* – if I must choose one in particular, Mme Isaac Pereire.

Alexander Walker

· LONDON
Author and cinema critic

The scent of flowers is for me like the taste of the *madeleine* for Proust. Flowers are for remembrance – of times past, places, moods, people, meetings and partings. Which is why I first think of *sampaguita*, national flower of The Philippines, small, white, jasmine-like in scent, strung on fine threads and hung round the necks of visitors to those marvellous Pacific islands. Small boys sell mini-chains of it in and out of the traffic jams; room-boys lay chaplets of it by one's bedside to ward off mosquitoes; beautiful girls do the formal honours with it at festivities, forcing one to bob and duck one's head under their encircling arms. For me, it is the scent of Shangri-la.

More evanescent and delicate, asking to be sniffed at instead of overpowering one's senses immodestly, is the *primrose*, flower of my Ulster childhood and tenderest of spring's early warning systems.

Fuchsia, too, is my link with home: not the ornate mutants of the hothouses, but the wild and bushy hedgerows of fuchsia all over the Mourne Mountains, turning scarlet as the wind rakes their olive outcroppings. I was raised in a town noted for nurseries of roses – McGredy's – though now it has only the gold medals enmeshed in the mayor's chair to recall the rosefields that once brought the place world-wide fame and prizes. My father had a charcoal-red rose named after him – Fred Walker – but even it's been rechristened into some generalized description to improve its international marketability.

But the rose isn't a favourite of mine: I prefer the *chrysanthemum*, Father's favourite too; for as I see our two greenhouses in my mind's eye, crammed with disbudded chrysanthemums as big as footballs, I see Father too, an awkward man in his oversized movements around the house, who became amazingly gentle as he cut his flowers at long last and put together the Christmas bunches we sent out to our friends . . .

Laburnum racemes I love for the blinding waterfall of sulphurous yellow – I remember seeing a whole laburnum tree growing indoors in the grey entrance hall of the stately home of Petworth, and thinking it far more wonderful than all the gaudy Turners on the walls . . .

For that sense of occasion it encapsulates, give me the *carnation*. the darkest red possible, as near to black as you can get. If only its calyxes weren't so resistant, or tailors were more pliable and made button-holes larger, the carnation would be the perfect 'man's flower'.

Anemones were my mother's flower – the delicate French kind, not the rawer Cornish variety. I still love to buy them when I am skiing in Switzerland, set them in a warm window niche and see the snowflakes drifting down for a backcloth. Always faintly Japanese, that scene, in some way I can't quite place, but maybe to do with those Christmas gifts of pressed Japanese paper flowers that expanded to huge and vivid dimensions when placed under water (whatever happened to this craft?).

Then give me simple field *daisies* and *dandelions*. The first I love to see in lawns and prefer an uncut carpet of daisies to the velvet-iest bit of turf; the second, because dandelion flowers turn into seed clocks and I still hanker to procreate the world with one puff. Weeds, yes: but looking at what unlovely things the architects have raised on sites once occupied by dandelions, I prefer weeds to urban renewal.

The *hollyhock*, preferably ten feet tall at least, is the one exotic note I love to find in cottage gardens. It is also the only flower that positively thrusts its seed pods at the covetous visitor to bear away and be propagated in his own patch back home. Fortunately, the bureaucrats haven't yet got round to telling us what we shall plant and where: if they do, the hollyhock will be the guerrilla leader. But all flowers resist dictatorship: they are the unofficial wonders of the world.

John Walker

LONDON

Former Director of the National Gallery,
Washington, DC

*Streptocarpus, roses, pansies, iris, lilac, poppies, clematis, wisteria,
hollyhocks, narcissi.*

Dame Rebecca West

LONDON

Author, critic and defender of justice

Meconopsis baileyi – the best blue ever; *paeonies* – preferably white
and scented; *iris stylosa* – nothing like a *large* patch of it for pro-
viding flowers for the house after New Year's; *daffodils* or narcissus;
delphiniums – deep blue and white; *irises* – preferably brown, and
brown and gold; *clematis* – with emphasis on spooneri; *aconites*,
in quantity; *pinks*; and, of course, *roses*.

Sally, Duchess of Westminster

WICKWAR, GLOUCESTERSHIRE

Gardener and traveller

You asked me to list ten of my most favourite flowers – those which
I would prefer to take with me to a deserted island on which I
presume I am to be stranded forever.

Well – the seasons really have always governed my enjoyment
of life so, to remind me of spring, I would crave *primroses* and
perhaps species *crocus* because it would be essential to have bulbs
and plants which seed themselves and increase into colonies.

Summer – most difficult to make a selection. Scent is of great
importance so I would plant *honeysuckle* to festoon my lair and
flowering mints and *herbs* to improve gastronomically whatever I
would find to eat (and to use medicinally if needed).

In the autumn and winter I might need shelter so why not an *apple tree* with that unbeatably beautiful blossom in the spring, anticipation of delicious and nutritious fruits to come, and dead wood from time to time to burn?

But how could I live without *lilies* and *roses*?

Morgan D Wheelock III

WESTON, MASSACHUSETTS
Landscape architect

You are very kind to ask me to participate and I am delighted because 'a house without flowers for me is abandoned'. They are very important to my life.

Anemone; *freesia*; *gardenia*; *cyclamen*; *tulip*; *cosmos*; *clematis*; *fuchsia*; *Oriental poppy*; *iris*.

Lady Widgery

LONDON
Wife of former Lord Chief Justice of England

Lily-of-the-valley; *primroses*; *roses*; *daffodils* – 'a host of'; *camellias*; *freesias*; *lilacs*; *paeonies*; *larkspurs*; *pansies*.

Emlyn Williams

LONDON
Actor and author

Alas (apart from enjoying exquisite flower paintings in the right hands!) I know *nothing* floral-wise; can just tell a rose from a bluebell and that's all.

I shrink from carnations, having had my first overpowering whiff of them at the age of eight in a small room containing an open coffin – but I doubt if this bit of information would enliven any flower game!

116

Lady Wilson

LONDON
Wife of the former Labour Prime Minister

Agapanthus lily (which is an African Lily which grows in my garden in the Isles of Scilly); *rose* ('Fragrant Cloud'); *lily-of-the-valley*; any variety of *daffodil* or *narcissus*; small scented *chrysanthemums* (not those huge curled ones); wild *cowslip*; meadow *daisy*; wild *bluebell*; wild *primrose*; wild *violet*.

As you can see, I have a preference for scented flowers.

Lord Wolfenden

WESTCOTT, SURREY
Educator and former Director
of the British Museum

Herewith my list, in alphabetical order after the first, which is clearly in a class by itself:

Fleur Cowles; *ceanothus*; *cyclamen*; *delphinium*; *fritillaria*; *hibiscus*; *oleander*; *passion flower*; *snapdragon*; *snowdrop*; *wallflower*.

And you can psychoanalyse that until you are blue in the face!

Michael York

LOS ANGELES
Actor

My list is influenced by both aesthetic and functional considerations. The last seven flowers on the list are noted for their excellent homoeopathic properties as well as their physical beauty and aromatic appeal. They would provide a balm for both spirit and body!

Gardenia; *orchid*; *freesia*; *dog rose*; *marigold*; *mimosa*; white *jasmine*; *primrose*; *iris*; *cyclamen*.

And, finally, a nod to a special flight of fantasy
from a very dear friend:

Pepe Mayorga

Madrid

My dear Fleur,

As I foresaw, when I first answered your letter inviting me to choose ten flower companions, El Romeral in Almeria has been the ideal location for thinking about your book: quite barren, desert-like and without any flowers, I was obliged to look up to heaven for guidance.

I cannot think of a book about flowers without reference to George Louis Leclerc, Comte de Buffon. Accordingly, I wrote to him and am pleased to enclose herewith copies of our correspondence for your consideration.

Hoping your book will enjoy the success it will undoubtedly deserve.

Pepe

Le Comte de Buffon,
Institut Botanique Celestial,
Le Paradis sur Cosmos

Madrid

Dear Count,

Unfortunately it is impossible to reach you by telephone. To visit you in heaven without the return guaranteed entails a price too high. I am left with my pen and here is my problem:

Like you, I have always enjoyed all flowers. I am not a bee, nor a butterfly. I have liked them as manifestations of beauty in nature. Since you departed, many new flowers have been hybridized which correspond easily to your classification. One only is different. It is called Fleur. Investigators think that it is the result of a celestial mutation induced to create the most beautiful flower in the world.

Imagine, dear Count, this beauty has had the idea to ask me which flowers I would choose to have with me all alone with nothing else on an imaginary island. I must choose ten. The more I think about it the more confused I become. My meditations lead me 'up the garden path' as your English admirers say, recalling, no doubt, your researches. Therefore, dear Count, I ask you kindly to advise me. We believe you have more leisure time up there and know better how to employ it. Besides, among so many angels you will not lack quills.

Pepe

Institut pour l'Investigation des Anges,
Le Paradis sur Cosmos

Dear Pepe,

What a pleasant surprise! I thought I had been forgotten despite all the research and hard work I left behind for the benefit of botanists. Here we do not have any plants, only angels . . . just like you with only flowers. Fortunately I have nothing to do with their selection. For some time I have been working on *The History of Angels*, to be published in 1985, two hundred years after my last book, *The History of Plants*.

As for your dilemma, having to choose from hundreds of thousands of flowers, I advise you not to think just on flowers; rather on the memories they evoke. Thus the imaginary island will be filled with the most pleasant souvenirs of the past, which after all represent the most indestructible capital one can have, either down there on earth or up here in heaven. The angels have none other and thanks to that their happiness is everlasting.

What your new Fleur proposes is, therefore, to establish for you personally a heaven on earth, which is a proof of her great friendship. I regret that she did not yet exist whilst I was down there amongst the flowers. But already I can classify her as 'Fleur Celeste' and I can foresee a great success at Chelsea. I will think of you on your little island, happy and grateful, in order better to merit the spirit of your friendship.

Buffon

Madrid

My dear Count,

You are unique! What a wonderful solution! I have always wanted to be rich and here, now, thanks to Fleur Celeste and to you, I am a wealthy man and this is my capital:

Fleur Celeste

Nasturtiums	Bougainvillea
Buttercups	Jasmine
Roses	Morning glory
Gardenias	Falling geraniums
Dahlias	Orchids

which correspond with the best memories of my life.

I am most grateful. It is unnecessary to wish anything for you. You are already in total happiness and you have been kind enough to lend me a little.

Pepe

The Most Popular Flowers

1	Rose	*159 votes*
2	Lily	*96 votes*
3	Lily-of-the-valley	*58 votes*
4	Paeony and Daisy	*56 votes each*
5	Lilac	*49 votes*
6	Jasmine	*47 votes*
7	Tulip	*44 votes*
8	Violet	*42 votes*
9	Poppy	*39 votes*
10	Daffodil and Orchid	*37 votes each*
11	Camellia	*36 votes*

The Most Popular Flower

The rose has not only conquered geography by its tenacity, as this book has proven, but all of man's emotions. How otherwise could it be infused with so many meanings sacred to religion and human love?

The symbolic rose, the mystical rose, is held like a benediction in the hands of painted saints and madonnas. It is the devout emblem of kings and queens. It is found in textured medieval tapestries, engraved on shields, even carried into battle. It is the delight of the troubadour. It personified sentiment to the Victorians – speaking of love of a decorous and deathless dimension.

It is a ballet: *Le Spectre de la rose* – when performed by Nijinsky in Monte Carlo, he made it immortal. As long as there was music, there were songs about roses – from folk songs to juke boxes to opera: Richard Strauss' *Der Rosenkavalier*. It is the written crest on the letters of Gertrude Stein: a rose is a rose is a rose. It is a jewel, translated into rings, brooches, tiaras, pendants and earrings in precious metals and diamonds. It is perfume, to which the wonderful Damask rose has devoted its life, expressly cultivated for perfume essences. It was once as tiny as an infant's palm, five flat petals in a colourful disc around a cup of perfume. From it, the city of Damascus got its name.

It can grow everywhere, defying all elements, even in a tin can (and sometimes becoming the size of cabbages) but it doesn't reject having a just share of care. Thorny by nature, serious botanists once claimed it was given its thorns as a weapon against crowding vegetation. Nonsense. Where isn't it seen in crowded collusion with other growing things (as alongside tomato plants during the War)? It is older than Eden, according to the Koran, which places it in the Garden of Paradise. It was the choice of ravenous Romans after conquests. Its petals covered their beds, litters, tables and the banqueting halls. Millions of petals were also strewn over streets. Even Cleopatra supplanted the lotus with roses, wearing garlands of them when Antony was near.

Whatever else the rose's history, special thanks must be given to Empress Josephine, who brought about its rebirth in Napoleon's time, in her gardens at Malmaison, living in the lap of luxury — where it was commissioned by the queen to be painted by Redouté, whose name jumps to mind when the word 'rose' arises. But I think also of Fantin-Latour and Cézanne, and so many other painters of flowers. No flower has served the painter better.

Pioneer women crossed the wilderness of the New World with their treasured rose seedlings and cuttings to plant as reminders of homes left behind; it probably also went as a precious companion to other women who faced the dangers of new lives elsewhere. Wherever carved in stone or marble or wood or embroidered on silks or painted on canvas or growing in an island garden, it is an homage of love: *the world's most beloved flower*.

Index of flowers, shrubs, trees etc.

Index of Players